VISIONING

HUMAN RIGHTS

in the New Millennium

Quilting
the World's Conscience

CAROLYN L. MAZLOOMI, PhD
Founder, Women of Color Quilters Network

Schiffer Publishing Ltd.

4880 Lower Valley Road · Atglen, PA 19310

Designed by Brenda McCallum

All photographs by Carolyn L. Mazloomi, with the exception of pages 64 and 68.

The text of the United Nations Declaration of Human Rights is © 1948 United Nations. Reprinted with the permission of the United Nations.

Front cover images: (*clockwise, from top left*) Viola Burley Leak, *No One Shall Be Held in Slavery*. Sharon Kerry Harlan, *We Are*. Sandra Scott, *Blood Ties*.
Back cover images: (*left to right*) Carolyn Crump, *Deeds, Not Words*. Wendy Kenderick, *Teen Tobacco Workers*. April Shipp, *The Waters Returned Him: In Honor of Aylan Kurdi, Age 3*.
Title page image: Carolyn V. Bunkley, *Article 14*. Page 6 image: Marion Coleman, *Living in the Shadows*.

Type set in Bitter/Angeline Vintage/Minion

ISBN: 978-0-7643-5740-4
Printed in The United States of America

Published by Schiffer Publishing, Ltd.
4880 Lower Valley Road
Atglen, PA 19310
Phone: (610) 593-1777; Fax: (610) 593-2002
E-mail: Info@schifferbooks.com
Web: www.schifferbooks.com

For our complete selection of fine books on this and related subjects, please visit our website at www.schifferbooks.com. You may also write for a free catalog.

Schiffer Publishing's titles are available at special discounts for bulk purchases for sales promotions or premiums. Special editions, including personalized covers, corporate imprints, and excerpts, can be created in large quantities for special needs. For more information, contact the publisher.

We are always looking for people to write books on new and related subjects. If you have an idea for a book, please contact us at proposals@schifferbooks.com.

Also by the Author:

And Still We Rise: Race, Culture, and Visual Conversations, ISBN 978-0-7643-4928-7

Other Schiffer Books on Related Subjects:

HERstory Quilts: A Celebration of Strong Women, Susanne Miller Jones, ISBN 978-0-7643-5460-1

Face to Face: Portraits of the Human Spirit, Alison Wright, ISBN 978-0-7643-4366-7

It is with warmest affection I dedicate this book to Shamim,
who is a constant source of joy in my life. You truly make my world
a better place in which to live.

Acknowledgments

I would like to offer special thanks to Sara Vance Waddell for your support of all my projects, and to Dr. Myrah Brown Green and Peggie Hartwell for their encouragement throughout this project.

Thanks to all the artists for their creative expression in the name of human rights.

CONTENTS

INTRODUCTION

DWELLING IN POSSIBILITY:
HUMAN RIGHTS IN AN UNJUST WORLD

"According to the United Nations, every human—just by virtue of being human—is entitled to freedom; a fair government; a decent standard of living, work, play, and education; freedom to come and go as we please and to associate with anyone we please; and the right to express ourselves freely."

Visioning Human Rights in the New Millennium is a call for action in the global struggle for human rights. Through artistic expression, utilizing the canvas of quilts, the artists here interpret the thirty articles of the Declaration of Human Rights.

The first recorded political recognition of human rights occurred in 539 BCE, when Cyrus the Great of Persia freed all slaves after he conquered the city of Babylon. Cyrus also declared that people in his kingdom had the freedom to choose their own religion. A clay tablet known as the Cyrus Cylinder listed each of his statements on human rights and is the first Declaration of Human Rights known to humankind.

The United Nations (UN) Declaration of Human Rights had its genesis on February 16, 1946, when the UN established a Human Rights Commission. Its establishment was precipitated by the horrific human rights violations suffered by victims of World War II. Eleanor Roosevelt was a member of the commission

and would go on to be elected its chairperson. Roosevelt brought to the table her compassion and commitment to human dignity, her empathy for the plight of the refugees of World War II, and her experience in politics and lobbying.

Eleanor Roosevelt's undertaking was a difficult one. Getting the nations of the world to unilaterally agree on one document for human rights was not an easy task. Finally, after two years of negotiations, the General Assembly of the UN adopted a resolution endorsing the Universal Declaration of Human Rights on December 10, 1948. The document represents the first global expression of rights to which all human beings are innately entitled, and stands to this day as the most widely recognized proclamation of the rights to which every person on our planet is entitled. Eleanor Roosevelt considered her role in crafting the Universal Declaration of Human Rights to be the most important accomplishment in her life.

Upon passing the motion to accept the Declaration, all the delegates rose to give a standing ovation to Eleanor Roosevelt—an elderly, shy woman with a very formal demeanor, quick wit, and warm smile. Ambassador Charles Malik of Lebanon declared: "I do not see how without her presence we could have accomplished what we actually did accomplish."[1]

Throughout the negotiations of the document, Mrs. Roosevelt soon found herself entangled in bitter confrontations with the Russians; however, they proved no match for her. She had determined

to complete the task at hand and drove her colleagues mercilessly. She had the delegates endure fourteen- to sixteen-hour days. It is said the delegate from Panama begged Mrs. Roosevelt to take pity on them and to remember that United Nations delegates have human rights too.[2]

During the summer of 1948, delegates finally saw the Universal Declaration take shape. Drawing on the French Declaration of the Rights of Man, the British Magna Carta, and the American Bill of Rights, Mrs. Roosevelt wanted a simple, eloquently written document.

Mrs. Roosevelt was proud of her role in shaping the Universal Declaration of Human Rights, but she was a realist. She knew that the Articles of the Declaration were not self-enforcing, and always told UN delegates that it was a matter of "actually living and working in our countries for freedom and justice for each human being." It was a challenge she enthusiastically accepted, and her example is forever inspiring. Mrs. Roosevelt is still one of the world's most admired and respected women.

Defined in the Declaration of Human Rights are four core freedoms vital to the progress of all human beings: freedom of speech, freedom of belief, freedom from want, and freedom from fear. All people are entitled to these rights, regardless of "distinction of any kind, such as race, color, sex, language, religion, political or other opinion, national or social origin, property, birth or other status." All human rights affect one another, and the violation of one right inhibits the actualization of others. The Human Rights Declaration is the most translated document in the history of the world and has been used as the founding document for many human rights organizations.

Amnesty International is one such organization that is based on the declaration; it is the world's largest grassroots human rights organization. People's human rights are abused and violated every day, and when this happens, Amnesty International finds the facts, exposes the problem, and gathers people together to force governments respect everyone's human rights. Amnesty International has helped

free the wrongfully imprisoned, fight for LGBTQ rights, and come to the aid of refugees, and has championed reproductive rights, free speech, and other critical human rights issues. In 1977 Amnesty International received the Nobel Peace Prize for its work on human rights.

The UN Declaration of Human Rights was also a model for the 1989 UN Convention on the Rights of the Child (UNCRC), created with the objective of safeguarding the lives of children around the world. The convention gives them access to things they need specifically because they are young, vulnerable, and still developing and cannot take care of themselves. The UN Convention on the Rights of the Child was adopted and signed by all the countries of the world, except Somalia and the United States. The introduction of the UNCRC has led governments to provide certain rights and services to children, has given them extra protections, and helps them should they find themselves in challenging or troubling situations. These situations include becoming refugees, being involved in war, or having committed a crime. The introduction and general acceptance of the UN Convention on the Rights of the Child has, without a doubt, improved the lives of numerous children around the world.

Indigenous people around the world have a common history of injustice. They are being killed, tortured, and enslaved. The UN Declaration on the Rights of Indigenous Peoples is also based on the UN Declaration of Human Rights and is the most comprehensive international instrument on the rights of indigenous peoples. It establishes a universal framework of standards for the survival, well-being, and dignity of the indigenous peoples of the world. It declares that indigenous people have a right to maintain their distinct social, legal, political, and economic institutions. Their cultural identity is protected and they are protected from genocide.

The Universal Declaration has served as a gathering point for individuals who are victims of oppression and human rights violations, such as Nelson Mandela in South Africa, Lech Walesa in Poland, Ai Weiwei in China, and groups of people such as those involved in the Me Too and Black Lives Matter movements. The Universal Declaration is the yardstick by which performance of the United Nations and nongovernmental organizations (NGOs) is measured, and has inspired more than twenty-five legally binding human right treaties globally.

I was inspired to write this book because of my admiration for Eleanor Roosevelt and my belief that if women were fully empowered, they would transform the world into a peaceful place. Every day, all over the world, women make peace between their children, their families, and their communities; however, when it comes to being included in negotiating and signing peace deals, they are excluded.

Women are sensitive to rights and human needs, and intergenerational perspectives. Mothers are natural nurturers, and the first teachers of their children. They are in a position to educate their children to value peace and not war. Women and their empowerment are crucial to advancing the culture of peace in all its vectors—education, sustainable economic and social development, human rights and equality, democratic participation, and advocacy based on true knowledge but also wisdom, tolerance, and understanding at all levels, in the family, community, country, region, and globally.

In a speech at the United Nations, Deputy Director Lakshmi Puri stated, "The realization and promotion of gender equality and women's empowerment is a way to deconstruct militarism, harmful masculinities, and patriarchy which exalt aggression and violence, and supports a culture of war in all its mad and irrational assault on humanity that we must end."[3]

Men, clearly, are traditionally more inclined toward war and conflict than women. I firmly believe that men are threatened by the power and spiritual strength of women and, in many cultures, don't want them educated. In some countries, men feel educated women infringe on their power hold over society and politics in communities and states. The abduction of schoolgirls in Nigeria is an example of how the empowerment of women and girls, their education and self-reliance, is in fact most threatening to the forces of violence and chaos by men, which is why the Taliban and Boko Haram attack, kill, or kidnap young girls as they learn.

So how can we eliminate war and construct a lasting global peace where all people can enjoy all facets of the Articles of the Declaration of Human Rights? Some spiritual teachings say that establishing equality between women and men can help lead the world to peace. "The world of humanity is possessed of two wings: the male and the female. So long as these two wings are not equivalent in strength, the bird will not fly. Until womankind reaches the same degree as man, until she enjoys the same arena of activity, extraordinary attainment for humanity will not be realized; humanity cannot wing its way to heights of real attainment. When the two wings or parts become equivalent in strength, enjoying the same prerogatives, the flight of man will be exceedingly lofty and extraordinary. Therefore, woman must receive the same education as man and all inequality be adjusted."[4]

In liberation struggles throughout the history of the world, arts activism has been central to the fight for human rights. The artists position themselves in the abiding tradition of using the arts to raise consciousness, voice social inequities, and build community. Artistic expression allows us to find, examine, and share what is within ourselves, how we view the world, and what changes are worth fighting for. The quilts shown in these pages are integral parts of our fight for human rights.

In *Visioning Human Rights in the New Millennium,* fiber artists render works that connect the viewer in an immediate visual dialogue with issues that might not otherwise be accessible, transcending language barriers and negotiating difficult topics with diverse audiences. The artists here engage viewers in human rights discourse in a powerful way.

The arts allow us to articulate and challenge oppressions and expand our imaginations. We quilt our joy, our struggles, our concerns, and our vision for a brighter future. Furthermore, the freedom to participate in arts and cultural work is itself a human right. Article 19 of the UN Declaration of Human Rights allows everyone the right to express their thoughts through any medium of their choosing. The right to experience, develop, and articulate our cultures is a necessary component of realizing the full range of human rights to which we are all entitled by virtue of being human. All people have the right to develop, participate in, and enjoy cultural lives. Article 27 of the Declaration enshrines the right of everyone to participate in the cultural life of the community in which they live.

Our worlds have become increasingly more interconnected, with new technologies changing the way we communicate. It is time we abandon the idea of "them" and "us" and begin to see humankind as one.

The objective of this book is to educate and inspire people to understand the meaning of human rights in its best practice, as well as human rights violations around the world, and the terrible consequences resulting from intolerance and bigotry. The artworks will encourage reflection and create dialogue around some of the most challenging human rights issues of our times. It is the goal of the participating artists to broaden the human mind by using art to communicate, engage, teach, and heal.

Many of the artists featured in this book have been creating quilts for decades and have been exhibited in many museums and galleries around the country. These artists are committed to their medium and craftsmanship and, more importantly, are interested in human rights issues affecting people around the world. Notably, many of the artists have felt the sting of discrimination in one form or another. Many have experienced violations of their human rights.

There is particular interest in certain Articles of the Declaration, which resulted in more than one quilt work on some topics. Of specific interest to African American quilters in this book are Articles 1 and 3 of the Declaration, which state that all human beings are born free and equal and are entitled to the right to life, liberty, and security. For centuries, peoples of African descent were subjected to the largest forced migration in human history as a result of the European slave trade. They have suffered racial discrimination and unfair treatment for hundreds of years. Unfortunately, racism has nor disappeared from the canvas of America and still makes life difficult for people of color.

The piece *Equality and Freedom Executive Order Proclaimed by the Source* by Mayota Hill, a woman of deep faith, speaks to freedom given by a higher power. The artist proclaims that the "source" of all life, God, by virtue of our birth, has made all human beings free.

In the quilt *The Lesson and the Equation* by Tierney Davis Hogan, the artist recalls strong life lessons given to her and her siblings by their father, who grew up in the rural segregated South. He instilled in his children the courage to stand up against racism and fight back not with violence, but respectful dialogue. Dr. Martin Luther King used methods of nonviolence throughout his leadership of the civil rights movement.

Several featured quilters are social workers and healthcare workers and have created work reflecting the theme of Article 25, which states that all people have the right to food and shelter. Mothers and children; people who are old, unemployed, or disabled; and all other people have the right to be cared for. Marion Coleman, a retired social worker, made the quilt *Living in the Shadows,* which depicts four scenes of despair: a mother and her hungry children, people in line to receive free food, a homeless couple sitting on a sidewalk, and a lone elder with no home to go to. The images are stark reminders that all people need to be cared for properly.

The image of a young woman sleeping on a park bench, with only newspaper shielding her body from the cold, was made by Valerie White. *Park Bench Rescue* addresses the fact that there are

more than 565,000 men, women, and children who are homeless in the United States. White's work calls attention to the shocking fact that the United States has the highest rate of homeless people of any industrialized country in the world.

Linda Ali, a retired pediatric nurse practitioner, pictures the solitary figure of a young girl crying. She used tear-shaped crystals on a hand-appliquéd figure to mimic tears. The title of the work is *A Crying Shame.* Ali brings to the forefront that many countries fail to take care of their greatest asset—the children. Oftentimes caregivers fail them, and laws don't always protect them. I am reminded that the United States is one of only two countries in the world that did not ratify the UN Convention on the Rights of the Child. That indeed is a "crying shame."

Many of the featured quilters are elementary school, secondary school, or college teachers and very much interested in the right of individuals to education, as indicated in Article 26 of the Declaration.

Plant a Seed by Beverly Smith shows five little African American girls, neatly attired in their school uniform, with books in hand, ready for a day at school. Ms. Smith is a public school teacher who teaches art in a middle school. Her pieces symbolize the importance of educating girls, because girls in many countries are denied the right to an education. Smith also emphasizes in her text the important role women play in raising children and helping their community, thereby making their education essential. Her statement also addresses the fear that men have of educated women, and how they seek to stop their education by harming them.

Hilda Vest made a quilt to honor Malala Yousafzai, the youngest person to receive a Nobel Prize. Malala was shot by the violent Taliban because she refused to stop going to school, and she spoke out against the Taliban's effort to force young girls out of the classroom. Malala has become an international symbol for the education of women and continues to advocate on their behalf.

Being able to read and write in the African American community has important significance. When enslaved Africans were brought to this country, they were not allowed to learn to read and write. In fact, there were laws in the South that declared that teaching an enslaved person to read was punishable by law. People could be fined or even placed in jail for the offense. Wendell Brown, a college art teacher, designed the quilt *Learning Always Instilled Freedom* to celebrate a long tradition of education in his family. The tradition was started by his great-great-grandfather, who was born the year slavery was abolished in the United States. Brown's hand-painted quilt illustrates the importance of going to school. The quilt shows young children and their teachers, dressed in their best clothes, ready to take a photograph on their first day of school. This "first-day picture" was a time-honored tradition at African American school in the South, as well as many others.

Human rights are much more than well-intentioned objectives set to legal language. It is imperative for society to live human rights through its practices, actions, and approaches. To live human rights values means to celebrate the diversity of our communities, support the oppressed, welcome the excluded, and be a voice for the voiceless. It is my dream that Mrs. Roosevelt's work was not in vain, and that all people can live in peace and harmony, enjoying the rights ascribed in the Declaration of Human Rights.

Carolyn L. Mazloomi

Notes
1. Bautch, Dana. "Eleanor Roosevelt: The Silent Minority." Columbia College, 1999.
2. Gardner, Richard N. "Eleanor Roosevelt's Legacy: Human Rights." *New York Times*, October 10, 1988.
3. Puri, Lakshmi. Speech at High-Level Forum on Culture of Peace at UN Headquarters in New York City, September 9, 2014.
4. Abdul-Baha. *The Promulgation of Universal Peace*. Haifa, Israel: Baha'i Universal House of Justice, 1982, p. 375.

THE UNITED NATIONS DECLARATION OF HUMAN RIGHTS

PREAMBLE

Whereas recognition of the inherent dignity and of the equal and inalienable rights of all members of the human family is the foundation of freedom, justice and peace in the world,

Whereas disregard and contempt for human rights have resulted in barbarous acts which have outraged the conscience of mankind, and the advent of a world in which human beings shall enjoy freedom of speech and belief and freedom from fear and want has been proclaimed as the highest aspiration of the common people,

Whereas it is essential, if man is not to be compelled to have recourse, as a last resort, to rebellion against tyranny and oppression, that human rights should be protected by the rule of law,

Whereas it is essential to promote the development of friendly relations between nations,

Whereas the peoples of the United Nations have in the Charter reaffirmed their faith in fundamental human rights, in the dignity and worth of the human person and in the equal rights of men and women and have determined to promote social progress and better standards of life in larger freedom,

Whereas Member States have pledged themselves to achieve, in co-operation with the United Nations, the promotion of universal respect for and observance of human rights and fundamental freedoms,

Whereas a common understanding of these rights and freedoms is of the greatest importance for the full realization of this pledge,

Now, therefore THE GENERAL ASSEMBLY proclaims THIS UNIVERSAL DECLARATION OF HUMAN RIGHTS as a common standard of achievement for all peoples and all nations, to the end that every individual and every organ of society, keeping this Declaration constantly in mind, shall strive by teaching and education to promote respect for these rights and freedoms and by progressive measures, national and international, to secure their universal and effective recognition and observance, both among the peoples of Member States themselves and among the peoples of territories under their jurisdiction.

ARTICLE 1.

All human beings are born free and equal
in dignity and rights. They are endowed with reason
and conscience and should act towards one another in
a spirit of brotherhood.

We Can Gather in a Circle

Jacqueline Johnson (Brooklyn, New York), 2016.
50 × 50 inches; commercial cotton, cotton batting;
machine pieced, appliquéd, and quilted.

If we can gather in a circle, talk to one another, and collaborate and
conspire for the greater good, there still exists a hope that we can
prevail against the conflicts of man against man, as reflected in our
local and international communities. If we can encounter each other
in the spirit of brotherhood, then all is possible.

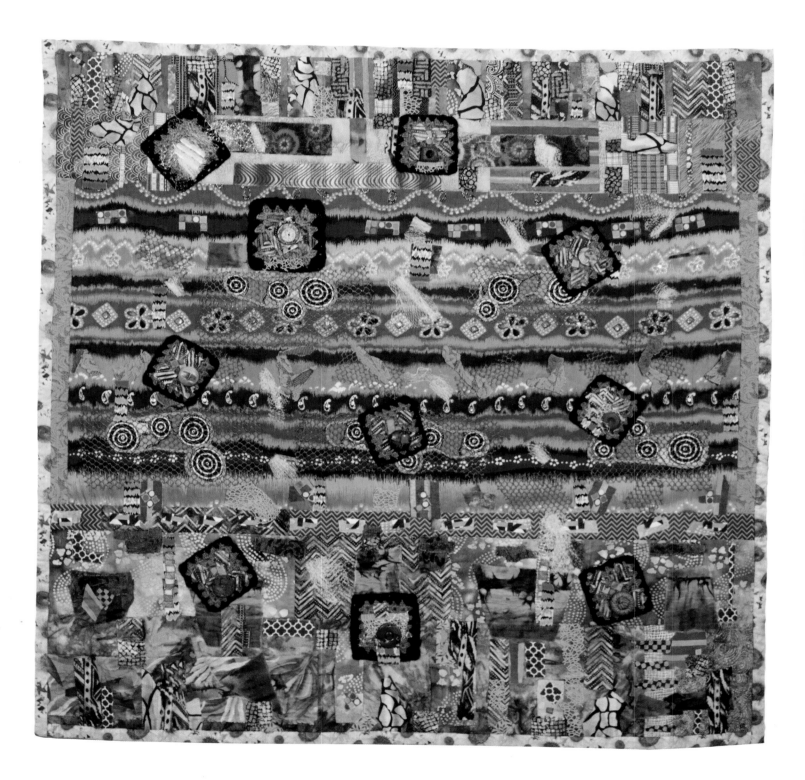

Equality and Freedom Executive Order Proclaimed by the Source

Mayota Hill (Pittsburgh, Pennsylvania), 2016.
50 × 50 inches, commercial cotton, cotton batting, buttons, found objects, machine pieced and quilted.

I was inspired to choose Article 1 of the Declaration of Human Rights: All humans are born free and equal because the act of birth automatically brings about the initial state of freedom—the act of breathing. Inhalation and exhalation is not a performance that is up for consideration to determine life but is a "given," which is irrevocably applicable to us all. Breathing is solely orchestrated and directed by the "SOURCE" and not man.

The Lesson and the Equation

Tierney Davis Hogan (Bend, Oregon), 2016.
50 × 50 inches, commercial cotton, cotton batting, appliquéd, machine pieced and quilted.

Article 1 of the Universal Declaration of Human Rights resonates the values that my father instilled in my siblings and me as young children.

My father grew up in the segregated South in the 1940s and embraced at an early age the belief that change comes from respectful dialogue, not violence.

He taught us that regardless of what adversity we faced in life, we must face it with grace and treat others with respect, dignity, and brotherhood. The foundation for a life lived embracing the values illustrated in Article 1 begins at home, modeled and mentored by the adults in a child's life (The Lesson).

In this quilt, a father (modeled after my own father in the 1970s) is teaching his children, on the main blackboard, the Equation to achieving a world in which people are Free and Equal:

Reason + Conscience = Spirit of Brotherhood.

The two individual blackboards, "Dignity" and "Respect," are the building blocks of the Free and Equal equation.

I am from a family of educators, beginning with my great-grandfather. The blackboards in the quilt honor that legacy.

My father also taught us another key lesson, which is best expressed in the words of Mahatma Gandhi: "I will not let anyone walk through my mind with their dirty feet."

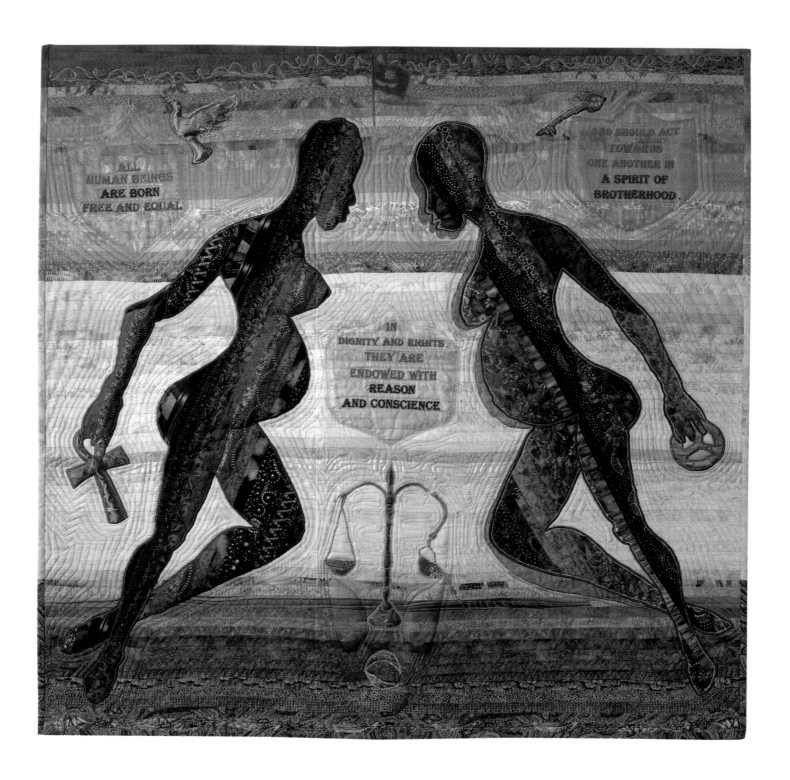

Construct, Power and Tare

Valerie Poitier (Massachusetts), 2017.
50 × 50 inches commercial cotton, cotton batting,
stripped pieced, machine appliquéd and quilted.

I reexamined pre– and post–World War II events to gain a fresh understanding of what led up to the formation of the United Nations and its declaration. As an elder, my understanding of displacement, expulsion, and wholesale murder of millions of human beings during WWII had grown and changed.

I began to fashion this story by looking for symbols of peace, protection, freedom, justice, equality, and human rights. I read Article 1 every day. I wanted the words in my conscious thoughts available to sink into every choice and every stitch. The goal was to depict Article 1 in a context sixty-nine years after it was created.

I searched for a means to balance the male-dominated constructs that led to a second world war. I chose one of my sketches. When cut from the pieced fabric, the enhanced sketch developed into a powerful female presence containing an uplifting representation of life. I was now positioned to select the remaining images, and their placement became clear.

Politics, race, wealth, poverty, weapons, famine, and war all are Constructs and relate to Power. The parable of the Tare found in the Bible was a reminder that the enemy may be sowing weeds in your wheat fields while you are not paying attention (not voting, as a nation or individual) or are sleeping. Hence the use of the words Construct, Power, and Tare in the title. Tare is also defined as the weight of an empty container as would be used on a scale. My scale of justice has the face of a male with tears of gold leaking from one of its "eyes." The scale has a broken arm, which represents, in many ways, our universal systems of justice and the ever-present need to stand up for human rights.

ARTICLE 2.

Everyone is entitled to all the rights and freedoms set forth in this Declaration, without distinction of any kind, such as race, color, sex, language, religion, political or other opinion, national or social origin, property, birth or other status. Furthermore, no distinction shall be made on the basis of the political, jurisdictional or international status of the country or territory to which a person belongs, whether it be independent, trust, non-self-governing or under any other limitation of sovereignty.

Edward Bostick (Brooklyn, New York), 2016.
40 × 42 inches, commercial cotton, acrylic paint,
cotton batting, hand painted, machine quilted.

Eleanor

Eleanor Roosevelt, the longest-serving first lady in history, was instrumental in redefining and reestablishing the role and the position of first ladies during her time in the White House. But she was also an activist and used that role to help forge social, political, and cultural change as well as the respect for cultural diversity in our country and the rest of the world. One example of this was her work on civil rights issues and her championing of Miss Marian Anderson.

Miss Anderson had been rejected in her permit request to give a recital at Constitutional Hall in Washington, DC, due to color of her skin. This incident highlighted the deep-rooted racial inequality in American society, which some felt had to be confronted and addressed, and who was more capable of addressing this issue than First Lady Mrs. Roosevelt? On February 26, 1939, she and other members of the organization resigned their memberships with the Daughters of the American Revolution to protest this refusal. She then worked with the secretary of the interior, who personally invited Miss Anderson to give the recital

on the steps of the Lincoln Memorial on Easter Sunday 1939. It is reported that more than 75,000 people of all races attended the recital on that cold Sunday morning, and millions listened to it on the radio. She started off with "My Country 'Tis of Thee" and ended with the powerful and stirring Negro spiritual "Nobody Knows the Troubles I Seen."

She was the first African American and first woman to address social issues from the steps of the Lincoln Memorial, where twenty-four years later, Dr. Rev. Martin Luther King Jr. would tell the world about his "Dream." The small pushes for opening up society from people such as Eleanor Roosevelt led to a generation of change that we still feel today.

Black Lives Matter

Deanna Tyson (Cambridge, United Kingdom), 2016.
50 × 50 inches, African and commercial fabric, netting, cotton batting, machine appliquéd and quilted.

Black Lives Matter is my response to Article 2 of the United Nations Declaration of Human Rights. Everyone is entitled to all the rights and freedoms set forth in the Declaration, without distinction of any kind, such as race, color, sex, language, religion, political or other opinion, national or social origin, property, birth, or other status.

Liberty Leading the People by the French Romantic master Eugene Delacroix was a very controversial painting created to commemorate the political uprising in Paris in July 1830, which all classes and political groups, except the absolute monarchists, supported. It is the visual expression of man's right to fight for freedom, to stand with his brothers against oppression, and to demand equality.

I have used *Liberty Leading the People* as inspiration for my piece Black Lives Matter. In my quilt, the central, symbolic figure of Liberty is replaced by an equally powerful woman of color, representative of all women. She wears the Phrygian cap, a symbol of liberty during the French Revolution. Just as in the present day, women played a leading role in the street protests of the 1830 revolution.

The young patriot to the right of Liberty represents the downtrodden youth of the nation calling for recognition and their own civil rights. This figure becomes a child soldier enslaved by and a member of the Lord's Resistance Army. He is symbolic of all the world's children forced into combat, slavery, and abuse, desperately in need of the implementation of the UN Children's Charter of Rights.

To the left of Liberty, replacing the aristocratic figure in a top hat, runs a representative of the LGBT Rights movement. A butterfly, the very symbol of freedom, flutters around his hat. In his painting, Delacroix conveyed the unity of the people involved in the uprising by the variety of hats, berets, and caps.

My quilt is worked in African wax cloth collected from the West African countries of Senegal, Ghana, Nigeria, and the Democratic Republic Congo, and also the United Kingdom's Brixton market. For me, wax cloth symbolizes both the African diaspora and those countries that figured prominently in the transatlantic slave trade.

We Are

Sharon Kerry Harlan (Wauwatosa, Wisconsin), 2017. 50 × 50 inches, artist-rusted fabric, artist-designed screen print, painted, collaged, thread embellished, machine pieced, machine quilted.

We are all humans and deserve certain basic rights and opportunities without fear of discrimination. There should be no disparity in access, choice, or privilege. Globally, however, people continue to experience such human rights violations and inequalities as child labor, human trafficking, ethnic cleansing, forced sterilization, and denial of gay rights. These victims feel abandoned to their fates.

We are powerful. United, we can enact the political, social, and economic change that will ensure that equality and justice prevail for the masses suffering human rights violations and discrimination. Without thought, we ought to and indeed have an obligation to aid other women, men, and children in need.

We are—yes, everyone—entitled to equality. It is not merely our hope, but humankind's destiny.

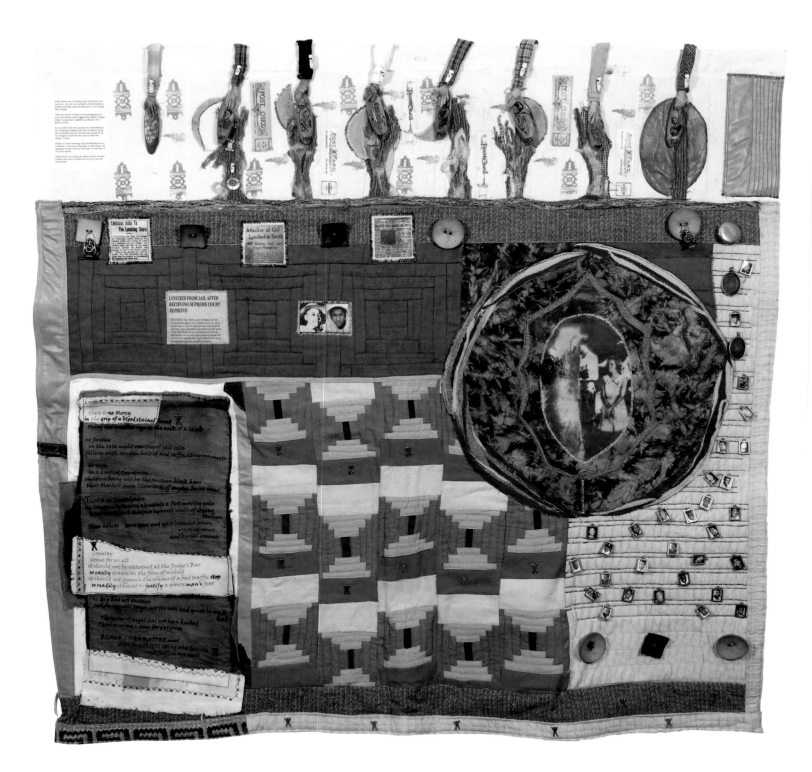

ARTICLE 3.

Everyone has the right to life, liberty and security of person.

Cruelty Come for Us All

James Mardis (Lewisville, Texas), 2015.
47 × 48 inches, recycled cotton, wood, metal framing, skull bone buttons, novelty found objects, linen, leather, clay, ink-dyed fabric, ink, shells, polyester, cotton and metallic threads, Pellon fusible fleece, collage, hand and machine sewn.

Cruelty Come for Us All is a multistory tapestry using a traditional patchwork quilt pattern: courthouse steps in two sizes and color schemes, with accented red courthouse doors, alongside appliqué, image transfer, fabric printing, thread and leather work with buttons, metal framing, and wood burning. Additionally, sleeved, clay-formed, blood-streaked hands top the piece in a grasping claim and introduction of the subject matter.

The tools and materials utilized in this piece are chosen to speak clearly to the harsh subject of America's familiar cruelties. Visually, the overused and blindly accepted terms of cruel lynching come to bear witness: Blood Moon, Lynching Tree, Courthouse Steps, Go Set a Watchman (lanterns), and Put Your Hands Up (metal figures) all come together for this experience and dialogue. Images of newspaper accounts and familiar totems (Martin and Till) carry forward the larger image that is also photodeveloped into the fabric of a small, white girl mimicking the lynched body of Rubin Stacey in 1937.

There is an original narrative poem on the piece that asks the question about the necessity of cruelty. Like the main image of Rubin Stacey, the poem is developed into the fabric like a found document with accents, utilizing an opposing color and fabric presentation, decorative stitching, and smearing techniques.

The entire right quadrant of the tapestry is a tribute and a caution to just sixteen of the growing myriad victims of what seems to be official cruelty by the police. Each image is duplicated and offers two versions of these victims: one image is slightly blurred, and the other is in full focus. Cruelty is often justified by confusion, and this feature introduces the idea of simply "taking a second look before you act."

Save the Children People of One Nation

Charlotte Hunter (Cincinnati, Ohio), 2017.
50 × 50 inches, commercial cotton, cotton batting, buttons, ribbons, sequins, braiding, cowrie shells, charms, found objects; machine pieced, machine appliquéd, and machine quilted by Sherry Vandervort.

Save the Children features three circular tapestries that reflect children of every nationality on earth. The children are depicted as flowers blooming throughout the world. The children carry braided banners depicting religious freedom, global peace, and human responsibility to provide food and shelter and to free the world of terrorism.

The braided banners suggest keys to achieve these global goals: respecting elders and cherishing the gift of knowledge. Even the Obama slogan suggests that these goals are achievable.

Caring hands stretch across the globe and continents and connect all nations. In the course of defending and seeking all human rights, the children must be taught to respect one another. They will be charged with responsibility for preserving our world, our planet, and our universe.

This quilt is dedicated to Carmen Mendez Lagdameo, who served as an executive secretary at the United Nations for decades for the Lagdameo Kids, who inspire the youth of the Philippines.

In gratitude to Rodolfo and Vilma Lagdameo, who diligently served the people of the Philippines, their native homeland, as well as the United States and around the world.

Right to Life

Arlene Jones (Bayswater, New York), 2017.
50 × 50 inches, commercial cotton, cotton batting,
machine appliquéd and pieced, machine quilted.

Article 3 states that everyone has the right to life, liberty, and security of person. Most countries have pledged to accept the Articles of the UN Declaration of Human Rights and have promised to protect and promote the rights of their citizens.

I chose to illustrate a group of youth at the public library studying the Declaration of Human Rights. National, state, and local governments create and provide free public libraries for all their citizens. Having access to a public library is an obligation and basic human right. The library is a center of learning where young people can learn the extent of this document on human rights, to understand all the freedoms they are entitled to. They can understand what a powerful document the declaration is. Once people are educated about their human rights, they become more-responsible citizens. Hopefully, knowledge about these rights will sow peace around the world.

Pink Vigilantes

Donna Chambers (Elmsford, New York), 2016.
50 × 50 inches, commercial cotton, cotton batting, painted, beads, netting, machine appliquéd and quilted.

My quilt tells the powerful story of the many despicable human indignities suffered by the women of India. My research began with an article in the *Huffington Post* titled "The Abused Indian Goddess." The article and its images raise awareness and campaigns against gender violence against women in India. Another article found in the Daily Beast introduced me to India's women warriors known as the Gulabi Gang. Gulabi, which means pink, inspired the quilt title The Pink Vigilantes. They are a group of female activists who wear bright pink saris as their uniform.

They fight for women's rights.

They fight for the abused women and children of India.

They fight against rape, prostitution, and sex trafficking.

They fight to feed and house the hungry and the homeless.

They fight to educate the Indian woman and end illiteracy.

They vow not to stop the fight against gender-based violence!

These activists carry sticks and fight to end India's widespread epidemic of domestic abuse against women. No woman of India is exempt from this horrible, often-fatal, intentional, gender-based violence known as femicide. I was deeply inspired to create and share this powerful story in fabric.

Behind the Mask: A Mardi Gras Indian at Home in New Orleans

Leni Levenson Wiener (New Rochelle, New York), 2016. 50 × 50 inches, commercial cotton, cotton batting, machine appliquéd and quilted. Based on a photo by Ellie Arbeit.

Outsiders. There are lots of them in lots of places; some seen, some unseen, and some choosing to remain unseen by masking their faces, either literally or figuratively.

The Mardi Gras Indians have historically been masked by choice. Upholding a tradition that dates back more than a century, they march in a ceremonial procession that was, until recently, hidden from the rest of the citywide celebration.

Named to honor the Native American populations who took in escaped and freed slaves immediately before and after the Civil War, these African American ceremonial "tribes" once used their costumes and masks to hide their identity and settle scores. Consequently, the Mardi Gras Indians were often associated with violence.

Today their parade and costumes are meant only to preserve and enrich their culture and its traditions. No longer considered outsiders, these residents of New Orleans have become part of the cultural fabric of the city; free to celebrate as they choose without fear of violence perpetrated against them.

The Inalienable Interrupted

Marlene O'Bryant Seabrook (Charleston, South Carolina), 2016.
50 × 50 inches, iPad-created imaged printed on cotton, commercial
cotton, cotton batting, printed fabric, machine appliquéd and quilted.

The Inalienable Interrupted is based on Article 3 of the Universal Declaration of Human Rights, which states: "Everyone has the right to life, liberty and security of person." This means that just by virtue of being human, we all have inalienable right to life, and to live in freedom and safety. The newspaper headlines and television reports do not seem to be in alignment.

Through this quilt, I am using my artistic voice to speak for voiceless children. While I strongly agree that all humans have a "Right to Life," I am focusing on young males on three continents: Africa, Asia, and North America, specifically the United States in the last case.

Like adults, young people across the world are promised by the UN Bill of Rights Declaration that their "Right to Life" will be protected. The normal expectation for children and youths is that they leave for school, play, and work, then return home safely at the end of the day. But at the time in their lives when their skies should be brightest, ominous and perennial clouds of vulnerability hang over some of them—especially the child soldiers of Africa and Asia, and to many preteen, teenage, and young adult black males in the United States of America. They constantly face their inalienable right interrupted by a bullet. The little boy represents, vicariously, all of the "at-risk" youths on three continents who just want to get home. It is my hope, one day, that the clouds will be behind them—a memory of the past social condition.

I used my iPad to create a painting of a male child riding a tricycle, maps/watercolors of child soldiers and Trayvon Martin, a newspaper, and topography. When I initially viewed the fabric printout, I noticed that, as expected, a word is the color of its background. "Home," on the sleeve of the hooded tee shirt, is the exception. It is colorless. First thought of as an easy-to-correct mistake, I quickly realized that it is a message. The right to arrive back home—alive—should not be based on color.

Teen Tobacco Workers

Wendy Kenderick (Gahanna, Ohio), 2016.
50 × 50 inches, commercial cotton, cotton batting,
machine piecing, appliquéd, and quilted.

After reading the United Nations Human Rights Declaration, I quickly settled in on Article 3, "Everyone has the right to life, liberty and security of person." Children are often left without a public voice and find themselves exploited for various reasons.

Teaching art to children has required me to be a better listener for my students, as oftentimes they need to be heard. My work *Teen Tobacco Workers* is inspired by Mexican muralist Diego Rivera and his painting titled *Sugarcane.* Mr. Rivera often addressed human struggle in his work and inspired me to give a voice to the children of immigrants caught up in the struggles of poverty. I have used the backdrop of my birthplace, Kentucky, where I first saw tobacco growing across the road from my aunt's house, for the images I have created.

Stop Violence against Women: Marissa Alexander

Dorothy Burge (Chicago, Illinois), 2016.
50 × 50 inches, commercial and hand-dyed fabric, machine appliquéd and quilted.

Marissa Alexander is a mother who was sentenced to twenty years in prison for firing a warning shot to protect herself from an abusive husband in 2012. Her case triggered outrage and sparked a national movement to protect survivors of domestic and family violence and sexual assault from being criminalized. Marissa, a mother of three, was released from prison and placed on house arrest in 2015. This quilt is intended to show her humanity and ignite compassion for her and other women and girls who must fight daily for their survival. Domestic and family violence is a human rights issue that disproportionately affects women and girls. It negatively affects a women's right to life, decent work, freedom of expression, education, and physical and mental health, and the right to be free from cruel, inhumane, and degrading punishment.

ARTICLE 4.

No one shall be held in slavery or servitude; slavery and the slave trade shall be prohibited in all their forms.

Latifah Shakir (Lawrenceville, Georgia), 2016.
50 × 50 inches, commercial cotton, satin, buttons, found objects, cotton batting, machine piecing, appliquéd, and quilted.

What You Took from Me

Love
I mean really
Love.

All the years I spent
placing blame on myself
When all those years
I should have blamed
someone else
for I was just a child
so innocent and vulnerable
I have now realized
I'm not the one responsible
for the act
that would destroy my
childhood
for the pain
that have meant me no good
for the silence
that has never been golden
for that moment
that was so early stolen.

What you took from me
Was something special
And it could never be
REPLACED
With nothing less than
Love.

—Akil Shakir

Slavery of the Twenty-First Century: Human Trafficking

Patricia Montgomery (Oakland, California), 2016.
50 × 50 inches, commercial cotton, cotton batting, ink, machine appliquéd and quilted.

For weeks, this quilt has been on my mind, and the key question was "How can I tell the story without the harsh sexual images associated with human trafficking?" After a week of early hours and meetings, I fell asleep at my desk instead of working on my meeting notes. In that brief moment, I saw the composition for this quilt. I sketched these gray abstract female forms that would play against a colorful background. These gray abstract female forms would represent the women and children forced into slavery of the twenty-first century. Suddenly, I remember all these words that described this kind of slavery. So instead of shocking images, I used the harsh words to tell the story about human trafficking.

Slavery was abolished 150 years ago, and yet there are more people in slavery now than at any other time in our history.

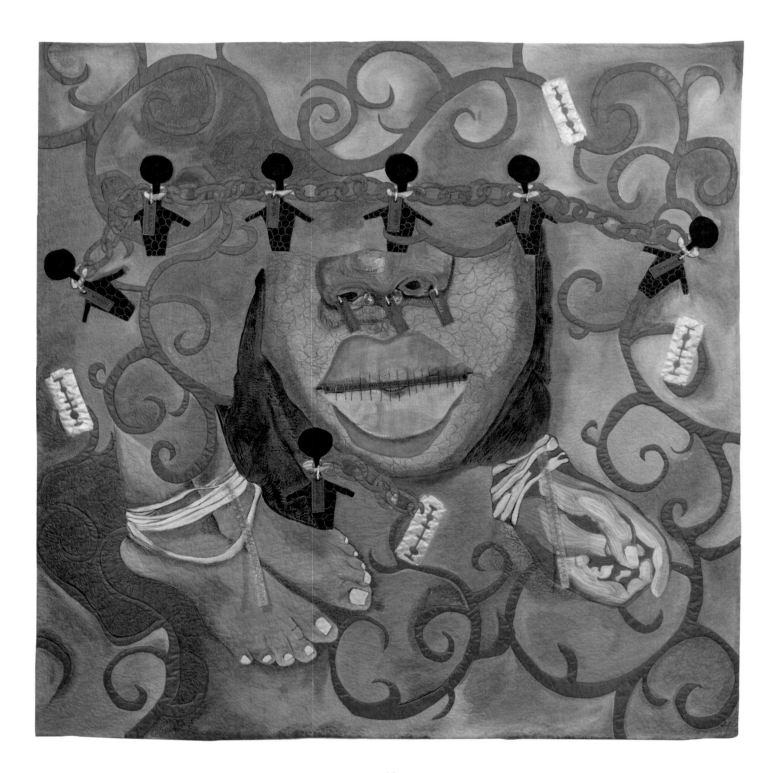

48

Blood Ties

Sandra Scott (Cambridge, United Kingdom), 2016.
50 × 50 inches, commercial cotton, cotton batting,
safety pins, metallic fabric, netting, acrylic paint,
machine appliquéd and quilted.

Blood Ties was created to highlight the issues of early childhood marriages, female genital mutilation (FGM), and the general mistreatment of young girls. It shows an incomplete face as the central image, with bound hands and feet beneath it. These recognizable symbols together are used to express the loss of identity and power for far too-many young girls who have no voice, and I have sewn the lips shut and covered them with the words "underage marriage equals slavery" to make this point. I have also stitched labels with these words attached to the bound hands and feet. I used chains, which are a universal symbol of slavery, to connect the black, simplified female symbols, each with name tags attached to the chain links. These tags are to give an identity to the faceless and unknown girls who have already gone through this ordeal, or to those who are going to be forced to go through it. I thought that by naming them I will somehow make them real and therefore help identify them as valuable human beings.

The razor symbol is used in my design to reveal their use in the brutal FGM ceremonies. One of the razors is attached to a link in the chain, illustrating that the societies are themselves slaves to this tradition. The beautiful swirls contrast with the blood-red color, showing that what is masked as a beautiful coming-of-age ritual is actually a violent abuse of a vulnerable child in the name of tradition.

No One Shall Be Held in Slavery

Viola Burley Leak (Washington, DC), 2016.
50 × 50 inches, commercial cotton, cotton batting, velvet, silk, machine appliquéd and machine quilted by Sue Moats.

This quilt references various forms of servitude, touching on slave trade in America, drugs, sex trafficking, blood diamonds in South Africa, and false imprisonment. Within this narrative are those waiting for release and those striving to climb to freedom.

ARTICLE 5.

No one shall be subjected to torture or to cruel,
inhuman or degrading treatment or punishment.

Helen Murrell (Cleveland Heights, Ohio), 2016.
50 × 50 inches, hand dyed cotton, cotton batting, acrylic paint;
hand painting, machine quilted.

Abolish Capital Punishment

I live in the United States, where Article 5 of the Declaration of Human Rights is not always applicable to all. The United States is one of the few remaining industrialized countries that practices the death penalty. My quilt, Abolish Capital Punishment, articulates my belief that the death penalty is a human rights violation not far removed from the lynching of black people. Most of the world has discontinued the practice of capital punishment; however, in some countries, poor and disenfranchised citizens are still executed by the state.

The stark background of the quilt is meant to evoke the atmosphere a prisoner may feel as that person awaits final punishment. The universal red "no" sign over two nooses leaves no question as to the message.

As I was making this quilt, I read that since 1973, 150 inmates were removed from death row because evidence had proven their innocence. But, I could recall only a few high-profile cases being discussed. These prisoners could have been killed because of an error, but that fact barely registers these days in our media-saturated society.

Although most of the world has discontinued the practice of capital punishment, there are twenty-two countries in which it is still legal. Nowhere has it been shown that the death penalty reduces crime or political violence. In many countries, capital punishment is used disproportionately against the poor or racial or ethnic minorities. As a violation of the fundamental human right to life, the time for capital punishment has come to an end.

I Am Not for Sale

Felicia Tinker (Cleveland Heights, Ohio), 2016.
50 × 50 inches, commercial cotton, cotton batting,
machine appliquéd and quilted.

This quilt was conceived by a grandmother of young people living in a city where children are reported missing daily. It was the angst and concern I felt that fueled the desire to bring attention to "human trafficking." I am that grandmother.

Human trafficking is the third-largest, multibillion-dollar illegal industry that seeks out men, women, and children for the sex trade. It is often referred to as a form of modern-day slavery. Sex traffickers usually seek out runaways, homeless youth, and social outcasts. Girls enter the sex trade between the ages of twelve to fourteen and are oftentimes romantically drawn into prostitution. This gross violation of human rights is a global problem; however, many are unaware that it is happening in their own backyards.

These infractions seem insurmountable, but I encourage you to join in the fight. Start in your community with awareness, learn the indicators of trafficking, and report any suspicions. The US Department of State has a list of ways you can help fight human trafficking. I believe that our children have the right to live in a healthy and safe environment, and I want victims to know that there is help. The National Human Trafficking Hotline is available 24/7. Its mission is to offer support, counseling, and a safe space for victims and survivors.

Now you know.

Your
Human
Rights
Are
Yours

I AM
NOT FOR
SALE

Healing Palms in Gilead: Jeremiah 8:21-22

Denise M. Campbell Sheridan (Atlanta, Georgia), 2017.
50 × 50 inches, commercial cotton, cotton batting,
machine appliquéd and quilted.

Article 5 of the Universal Declaration of Human Rights states: "No one shall be subjected to torture or to cruel, inhuman or degrading treatment or punishment."

During a six-month sojourn of ethnographic research in Belize, I witnessed many inspiring examples of cultural pride, community strength, and ingenious problem solving for complex issues confronting the Belizean people. One of the most compelling human rights challenges taxing Belizean resolve, as in other countries all over the world, is cruel, inhuman, and degrading sexual exploitation and abuse, especially involving young children. Combined with oral-history interviews, my research into this condition included reviews of the annual Belizean self-study *Belize Report on Human Rights* (2014–2016), as well as the US Department of State's *Trafficking in Persons Report* (2017). These government documents shine a penetrating light on this fundamental human right, as quoted below.

"There were anecdotal reports that boys and girls were exploited in child prostitution, including the 'sugar daddy' syndrome whereby older men provided money to young women and/or their families for sexual relations. Similarly, there were reports of increasing exploitation of minors, often to meet the demand of foreign sex tourists in tourist-populated areas or where there were transient and seasonal workers . . . The government did not effectively enforce laws prohibiting child sex trafficking" (*Belize Report on Human Rights*, 2016, p. 87).

Healing Palms in Gilead conveys the communal efforts of women, in particular, to use their hands in taking action to say no to sexual abuse perpetrated against them and their children. In circles of support on the palms of these women's hands, "No to Sexual Abuse" is translated into three languages commonly spoken in Belizean communities: English, Spanish, and Garifuna. One mother takes action to protect her child from this exploitation by cycling off the scene of the quilt, while young children look on, pondering their future fate. Just as the healing balm of Gilead provided hope for the biblical community cited in the Old Testament book of Jeremiah, the women of Belize, in solidarity with others across the globe, are providing healing hands (palms) for their families and communities.

My Dress, My Choice

Latifah Shakir (Lawrenceville, Georgia), 2016.
50 × 50 inches, commercial cotton, satin, buttons, found objects, trim, buttons, beads, pieced, cowrie shells, Tyvek, recycled denim, recycled antique quilt, cotton batting; machine piecing, appliqué, and meditative hand stitching, machine quilted.

Women should have the right and power to choose what is best for their bodies and dress. Genital genocide against women of Africa and the Middle East is considered a respected tradition. These rites of passage strip girls and women of their dignity and respect. The practice leaves women with a lifetime of unbearable physical and emotional pain, and I consider it torture. Laws have been enacted in some countries to prevent FGM (female genital mutilation); however, the law has been grossly ignored by the men and tribal traditionalists, so these rituals continue to be practiced. Women are getting fed up with ancient rituals and want a voice in saying "No" to violence, gender injustice, and torture.

59

De Luto—
in Mourning

Sylvia Hernandez (Brooklyn, New York), 2017.
50 × 50 inches, commercial cotton, cotton batting;
machine pieced, appliquéd, and quilted.

I made this quilt in honor of the forty-three Mexican students who disappeared on September 26, 2014, from Ayotzinapa, Mexico, while on a social-justice school trip. It was part of an ongoing exhibit titled *Tribute to the Disappeared / Tributo a Los Disaparecidos*. The theme is victims of injustice around the world.

Rose Green (Cincinnati, Ohio), 2016.
50 × 50 inches, commercial cotton, cotton batting,
machine appliquéd.

Bride Burning

This quilt is my expression of how I feel about women in India and how they are sometimes treated. I could not begin to imagine having a husband torture me through bride burning or throwing acid in my face because he no longer wanted me as his wife. The devastation of pain, both physically and emotionally, is degrading and leaves the victim forever scarred and traumatized. The women often have little legal recourse against their spouses. The depression wears on the soul of the victim(s), leaving very little hope of any kind. As I created the look of fire on my quilt, I felt sad and disheartened. I then began to feel consumed with anger at the thought of any woman enduring such torturous treatment. I pray that such abusive treatment ends soon, and that its victims are given new hope.

ARTICLE 6.

Everyone has the right to recognition everywhere as a person before the law.

Going Beyond the Self: Lale and the Omo Children

L'Merchie Frazier (Boston, Massachusetts), 2016.
50 × 50 inches, tulle, cotton batting, layered college, and quilted.

While viewing a series of TED talks, I came across one that was truly intriguing that featured a casually dressed young man who spoke very seriously about an issue concerning children in his home in the Omo Valley of Ethiopia. This quilt celebrates the amazing true story of Lale Labuko and his journey, despite the odds of personal danger, to protect the lives of children, to bring a progressive cultural shift in his village, and to confront his own death and the elders about the traditional practice of *mingi*. He raises the bar of humanity to protect the lives of the children affected by this practice, acknowledges their rights as persons, convinces the elders to change the practice, and obtains the protection of the Ethiopian government to protect them by law.

Lale Labuko, born and raised in the Kara tribe in the Omo Valley, Ethiopia, learns of *mingi* at age fifteen. Children born out of wedlock, those whose top teeth grow in before their bottom teeth, and even those who are born a twin are killed by virtue of this ancient tradition that deems them *mingi*, or cursed. Lale strives not only to save these children's lives but also to lift the "burden" from the shoulders of the Kara people; he adopts these children as his own. Lale attempts to reconcile with Kara elders to end this tradition forever in order to ultimately protect the longevity of his people and his culture.

Lale's journey, where he confronts his own death, negotiates deeply rooted superstition and navigates the difficult position of leading a cultural movement through his Omo Child Foundation. The quilt narrative embraces the image of a young black man caring for children, juxtaposed to the popular images that frame violence as the reference. I am simply in awe of the conscious effort and action that Lale "pays forward."

ARTICLE 7.

All are equal before the law and are entitled without any discrimination to equal protection of the law. All are entitled to equal protection against any discrimination in violation of this Declaration and against any incitement to such discrimination.

Dorothy Burge (Chicago, Illinois), 2016.
50 × 50 inches, commercial and hand-dyed fabric, machine appliquéd and quilted.

I Matter

The Black Lives Matter movement was created in response to the killing of Trayvon Martin in 2012. Trayvon was a seventeen-year-old African American male who, while returning home from a local store, was shot and killed by a neighborhood watch volunteer. I was moved by Trayvon's death because I realized that this could have happened to anyone of my young family members. This realization caused me to participate in many forms of activism to fight for justice for Trayvon. I signed petitions to the courts and elected officials. I marched in rallies and held teach-ins on the shooting and the legal issues surrounding the criminal case. I also created an art quilt, *Trayvon Could Be My Son*, which became part of the *And Still We Rise* quilt exhibit, created by an international group of artists from the Women of Color Quilter's Network and curated by Dr. Carolyn Mazloomi. The original quilt was inspired by one of my great nephews who was the newest addition to our family. Four years later and after another new addition to the family, I am committed to continue the fight to protect the human rights and dignity of black lives and to let our children know that their lives do matter.

Target Series: We Matter

L'Merchie Frazier (Boston, Massachusetts), 2016.
50 × 50 inches, nylon, cotton batting, layered college,
machine quilted. Photo by Craig Bailey–Perspective Photo.

We all have rights, no matter where we are. The Target series is an ongoing series of works that are designed to pose a counternarrative or pose questions that address the dominant narrative imposed on targeted populations. The term "target populations" refers to the entire group of individuals or objects about which researchers focus and generalize their conclusions, as determined by a selected set of socioeconomic criteria. These populations as individuals, families, neighborhoods, and communities are composed of demographics that are under the microscope, with issues defined by the researcher or organized agencies. In many instances, those observing and surveying the target group build messages to label the group that are explicit and implicit about that group. Examples of targets in our communities are young black men and women, groups mislabeled "terrorists," and other labels that select and define neighborhoods with negative inferences, survey results, and trumped-up data.

We Matter is my response and counternarrative to the focus on youth of color in our communities and the world. The target spirals reverberate a duality of aim and also a response from the targeted, the transformed holler, and the zone of sound. I chose the layers of colors and features to indicate the complexity of identity. My questions: What are the variables to determine the target? What are the credentials? Who has the power?

Justice Prevails

Dr. Cleota Wilbekin (Cincinnati, Ohio), 2017.
50 × 50 inches, printed cotton, machine quilted.

Article 7 of the United Nations Declaration of Human Rights states that every person is equal before the law, and everyone must be treated the same. The law must be impartial and fair to all. Neither privilege, race, nor religion should influence that justice. As an African American lawyer, I have witnessed inequality of the justice system in the United States firsthand. Whether African American men are perpetrators or victims, they aren't necessarily always given a fair shake in the American justice system. African American men receive longer sentences, are imprisoned at seven times the rate of whites, and receive the death penalty more often. In large cities throughout America, African American men and women are stopped by police, often without cause. My quilt is a kaleidoscope of the scales of justice. It is my hope that the scale is balanced for everyone, and not tipped in favor of anyone because of race, color, or creed.

Quilt submitted posthumously on behalf of Dr. Cleota Wilbekin, 1930–2017.

So What Skeletons Are in Your Closet?

Ed Johnetta Miller (Hartford, Connecticut), 2016–2017.
50 × 50 inches, commercial cotton, photo transfer, cotton batting; machine pieced, appliquéd, and quilted.

I lived through the civil rights movement and was always struck by the hatred and animosity shown to us by white people in the South—the crowds that gathered to spew hateful chants and throw eggs and thrash at African American children who were integrating schools. I recall reading the book *Without Sanctuary: Lynching Photography in America* by James Allen and John Lewis and seeing hundreds of gleeful whites—men, women, and children—attending the lynching of African Americans. Watching the charred and mutilated bodies swinging from trees. I often wonder where those people who took such pleasure in our torment and pain are. Where are they? Do they have remorse? Do their children and grandchildren know about their racist behavior, or do they hide these skeletons in their closet?

Lady Justice

Marian Coakley (Detroit, Michigan), 2016.
50 × 50 inches, cotton batting and thread, commercial cotton, machine appliquéd and quilted.

Justice is said to be blind, unbiased, and true. But is it? Lady Justice represents all that is right and virtuous within the legal system. She is, however, sometimes bound, gagged, and withheld from the truth.

ARTICLE 8.

Everyone has the right to an effective remedy by the competent national tribunals for acts violating the fundamental rights granted him by the constitution or by law.

Lauren Austin (Ann Arbor, Michigan), 2016.
50 × 50 inches, hand-dyed and hand-blocked cotton fabric, cotton batting, machine appliquéd and quilted.

Parole Denied

Parole Denied is about the parts of the US judicial system hidden from public view. I want to always remember the women behind bars, and their resistance against a system that denies them any hope. I created this work to remember my visits to people in prisons and jails—and to acknowledge the denial of human rights and the denial of humanity in the strange ways of the visitation rooms, parole boards, and jail and prison administration.

Visually this piece started out as a study of prison-visiting day, remembering how mothers would wait with their backs to the windows, turning around only when they heard the voices of family members. How it seemed like no one wanted to be watching when no one of their family appeared. Also seeing the children in that window, eagerly looking for their mothers, happy and sad at the same time.

Then I considered the arbitrary parole process, so like the lottery where the dream is never realized. Is it just a cruel joke? The crumpled letter in the corner is one of Debbie Sims Africa's many parole denial letters I found on the internet. The story of MOVE in Philadelphia is so old (1985), yet so shocking, still. Debbie is a grandmother now and, with the remaining members of the Move 9, continues to be incarcerated beyond her sentence for steadfastly maintaining her innocence. The

most difficult part of the work as an artist is, How do you visualize a right? The idea of true justice coming from this US legal system is impossible for me to "see." Even though I have lived a long life, practiced law, and made art throughout, I have never seen the rights articulated by Article 8 of the UDHR. People of color—and cis/trans women of color especially—have never had these rights. So how am I to create art about something I have never seen?

We often focus on the abuse of rights in other countries, to silence the voices at home that speak uncomfortable truths. It is easier to discuss human rights abroad than to confront it at home. I lived abroad for many years and always felt it was not for me to critique and theorize about rights or democracy in place of the people who live there. It is for me to do the critique and to take action in my own country. I feel solidarity with all human rights activists around the world, but my speaking out must be about my own people and my own country. When everyone is given safe space to speak for themselves, no one will need to speak for them.

I want to speak to destroy silence and invisibility. I draw in bright colors and write in bold letters for the legion of sisters erased by incarceration, and to strengthen the connection between international human rights and the struggle to stay alive in our country that is not our country.

ARTICLE 9.

No one shall be subjected to arbitrary arrest, detention or exile.

Say Her Name

Lauren Austin (Ann Arbor, Michigan), 2016.
50 × 50 inches, hand-dyed and hand-blocked cotton fabric, cotton batting, machine appliquéd and quilted.

I am mindful of all the visual art generated by the Black Lives Matter movement. I acknowledge that work by creating something different. Say Her Name is my meditation on our human rights, instead of showing our people either being killed or protesting the killings. The images of violence against black people saturate our atmosphere—they are with us at every turn and will not let us be. We cannot respond deliberately with so much noise directed at us.

Instead I aim to bring myself into a meditative state that will get me ready to move, to resist, and to make change. It is a quiet place, heavy with resolve, perseverance, and a sense of history. The figure here wears my mother's blouse because I often observed her in this state, especially before going into action in her hard, revolutionary work. I wanted to re-create that state of being.

I used the internet to research black cis/trans women killed by law enforcement. This led me to the excellent report "Say Her Name: Resisting Police Brutality against Black Women," by the African American Policy Group and its director, Kimberlé Crenshaw.

I read about each woman and girl killed extrajudicially who is listed in my quilt. The theme running throughout was to shoot first and ask no questions. Hasn't this always been our story?

I found myself screaming and crying and shaking at each outrage. The names of women and girls killed extrajudicially by police in the US up until I finished the piece are included along the outside edges. The oldest woman in the group was ninety-two years old and the youngest was seven at the time of their deaths. The title is from the #SayHerName critique developed within the Black Lives Matter movement to bring forward the names of black women who were also killed by police. I also looked up local news articles, funeral programs, and Facebook pages on each woman. I wanted to be sure they were not invisible to me or to the viewers of my work. I wanted to say their names. I say their names here. Say their names.

Our lives fall as spring leaves, before their time.

Detainment

Sandra Noble (Warrensville Heights, Ohio), 2016.
50 × 50 inches, cotton fabric and batting, machine appliquéd and quilted.

Detainment perpetuated worldwide is synonymous with captivity, internment, and incarceration.

I chose unfair detainment as the focus of my quilt because of my concerns of the inhuman escalation of how man treats other men through detention. My interpretation of unfair detainment is another way of saying "having power over the powerless"—oppression.

Human trafficking attracts all races, genders, and ages for the purpose of forced labor and prostitution. It occurs from the United States to the Sudan, from India to Argentina, from Sweden to Afghanistan—it is worldwide.

There is documented evidence of local police and governments arresting people not only for committed crimes, but also based on the color of their skin or their perceived religion. Being black or Muslim in some parts of the world is like waving a red flag to some law enforcement, which can lead to arbitrary arrest and being charged without real evidence.

Finally, I think that immigrant camps are cruel places for people who are already suffering, displaced from their homes because of poverty, war, and terrorism. Some immigrant internment camps are surrounded with barbed wire fences, which look like prison camps. The people within are treated like criminals. Immigrant families face homelessness, hopelessness, and fear of the future.

ARTICLE 10.

Everyone is entitled in full equality to a fair
and public hearing by an independent and impartial tribunal,
in the determination of his rights and obligations and of
any criminal charge against him.

Carolyn Crump (Houston, Texas), 2017.
50 × 50 inches, hand painted, commercial fabric,
cotton batting, machine appliquéd and quilted.

Waiting to Have My Say

African Americans often fail to get a fair trial in court when accused of a crime in the American justice system. The aphorism "innocent until proven guilty" does not apply. Early in American history, angry white mobs used violence as their own form of "justice" and carried out thousands of lynchings. The presumption-of-innocence doctrine has been described as the foundation of fairness in the American legal system: a system designed to protect innocent citizens from wrongful conviction. Most white people automatically associate a black with being guilty, and a white face with being not guilty. America's prisons are filled with African Americans who don't belong there. Many have also been executed on the basis of false evidence.

Although the right to a fair trial is accepted by many nations as a fundamental human right, and most countries are required to respect it, such is not always the case, especially for those seen as the minority. In an ideal world a jury is the key element of due-process protections, the voice of community values, and the guardian of the public trust. African Americans have, for the entire history of the United States, faced a legal system that treats them far differently than its white citizens. It is my hope that this issue will one day change, and all citizens are treated equally in the eyes of the law.

ARTICLE 11.

(1) Everyone charged with a penal offence has the right
to be presumed innocent until proved guilty according to law
in a public trial at which he has had all the guarantees
necessary for his defense.
(2) No one shall be held guilty of any penal offence
on account of any act or omission which did not constitute a penal
offence, under national or international law, at the time when it was
committed. Nor shall a heavier penalty be imposed than the one that
was applicable at the time the penal offence was committed.

Jim Smoot (Chicago, Illinois), 2016.
50 × 50 inches, hand painting on cotton,
acrylic paint, hand quilted.

J'Accuse

J'Accuse is my visual interpretation of "we're always innocent till proven guilty." Nobody should be blamed for doing something until it is proven. When people say we did a bad thing, we have the right to show it is not true. My depiction shows an unseen accuser, and a metaphorical victim under real or perceived confinement.

No one shall be subjected to arbitrary interference
with his privacy, family, home or correspondence,
nor to attacks upon his honour and reputation.
Everyone has the right to the protection of the
law against such interference or attacks.
United Nations   Art. 12
Right to Privacy

ARTICLE 12.

No one shall be subjected to arbitrary interference with his privacy, family, home or correspondence, nor to attacks upon his honor and reputation. Everyone has the right to the protection of the law against such interference or attacks.

The Right to Privacy . . . Big Brother Is Watching

Theresa Polly Shellcroft (Victorville, California), 2016.
50 × 50 inches, commercial cotton, machine appliquéd and quilted.

The challenge of addressing the UN's statement on the Right to Privacy required soul searching. It is pleasing to know that the UN members consider these rights important by taking a stand confirming them worldwide. With the establishing of these rights comes also the need for security, which is being practiced through surveillance. The term "Big Brother" came to mind. We, members of the greater world community, are under constant surveillance. We cherish our right to privacy in our homes, in our communications, and in our religious practices, as we travel and as we explore the world of the internet.

This quilt is to celebrate our right to privacy without "arbitrary interference" as expressed in the UN statement and as written on this quilt. Each of the quilt vignettes reminds us of our rights. The question being addressed in this work is the concern for privacy with the day-and-night gaze of Big Brother, symbolized by the Eye, almost invisible here. Where does the right to privacy begin and end? Big Brother is watching! Is Big Brother watching to protect or is it interference with those rights?

ARTICLE 13.

(1) Everyone has the right to freedom of movement and residence within the borders of each state.
(2) Everyone has the right to leave any country, including his own, and to return to his country.

The Monarch Butterfly

Deanna Tyson (Cambridge, United Kingdom), 2016. 50 × 50 inches, African cotton, commercial cotton netting, cotton batting, machine appliquéd and quilted.

The *Monarch Butterfly* quilt is my response to Article 13 of the United Nations Declaration of Human Rights, which declares our individual right to freedom of movement, which has particular resonance in our present troubled world, not only concerning the Mexican-US border but also the huge migration of refugees from the Middle East to Europe.

The monarch butterfly is famous for its seasonal migration between Canada and Mexico. Migration is built into the monarch's DNA. The butterfly is also symbolic of freedom, of the right to roam. So for these very reasons, this beautiful, bright, orange-and-black butterfly has been appropriated as a symbol in the political action of Mexican migrants. The butterfly appears painted on walls and on billboards and is printed on posters, buses, and T-shirts as part of the "Migration Is Beautiful"

campaign, while migrants themselves don cardboard butterfly wings to protest against the borders and barriers they encounter.

My *Monarch Butterfly* is created from African wax cloth from Senegal and the Democratic Republic of the Congo. The ensnared, despairing migrant is molded from tapa bark cloth from Tonga. He sits ensnared by barbed wire and trapped behind a netting fence, his free passage blocked. The migrant's torn and tattered wings bear images of a past life lost, of happier times with mothers, wives, and families, all aspects of life sorely missed in his lonely struggles and exhausting expedition to the Promised Land.

Everyone may have the right to freedom of movement; however, that "right" is frequently ignored.

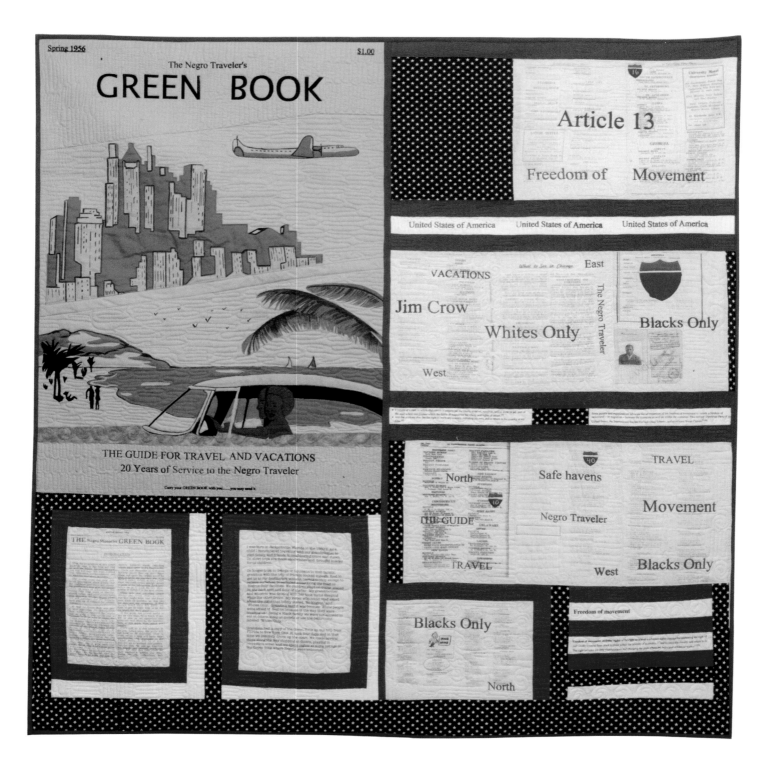

The Green Book

Ife Felix (New York, New York), 2016.
50 × 50 inches, photo transfer on cotton,
machine piecing and quilted.

I was born in Jacksonville, Florida, in the 1950s. As a child I remembered traveling with my grandmother to visit family and friends in neighboring cities and states. On short trips she made sandwiches and brought snacks for us children. On longer trips to Georgia or Louisiana to visit family, Grandma, with the help of friends, cooked enough food to get us to our destination without having to stop except to relieve ourselves in secluded areas along the road or "Negros Only" facilities. We children slept on quilts placed on the back seat and floor of the car.

My grandmother and whoever was driving with her took turns sleeping while the other drove. My sister, who could read, asked about the signs that boldly stated "No Negros" and "Whites Only." Grandma said it was because "white people are afraid of Negros because of the way they treat us." Because we were a black family, we were not allowed to eat at diners, sleep at motels, or use the bathrooms labeled "Whites Only."

Grandma had a copy of the book commonly known as the Green Book on our trip from Florida to New York City. *The Negro Motorist Green Book* was a guide to help African American travelers find businesses, shelter, food, and services during trips away from home. It was only after the passage the Civil Rights Act of 1964 that the Green Book ceased to be published, because there was no need.

Our trip took four days, and in that time we leisurely drove up the coast. African Americans suffered difficult times traveling during segregation. We made several stops along the way, stopping at diners and playing in recreation areas, and we spent nights at some listings in the Green Book where Negros were welcomed.

ARTICLE 14.

(1) Everyone has the right to seek and to enjoy in other countries asylum from persecution.
(2) This right may not be invoked in the case of prosecutions genuinely arising from non-political crimes or from acts contrary to the purposes and principles of the United Nations.

The Waters Returned Him: In Honor of Aylan Kurdi, Age 3

April Shipp (Rochester Hills, Michigan), 2016. 50 × 50 inches, commercial and hand-dyed cotton, velvet, monofilament, poly batting, plastic, leather, buttons, machine pieced and appliquéd, machine quilted.

There they were. The shocking images of a young boy's body washed ashore on a beach in Turkey. Plastered across the evening news. I stared at my television in disbelief. This was someone's baby boy dressed in a red shirt and blue shorts, lying lifeless on the sand. My heart was heavy. It takes a mother to know a mother's heart, and my heart was broken. I can't image moving from city to city to escape a civil war. I can't image the desperation of having to flee my homeland with my family in the middle of the night. I can't imagine being packed with fifteen others on a boat designed for eight, without a single life jacket. Can you?

I chose to machine-piece fabrics to represent an aerial view of the Al Zaatari refugee camp in Mafraq Jordan near the Syrian border. The refugee camp is home to more than 80,000 people who fled Syria. The cupped hands represent the ocean. They cradle little Aylan Kurdi's tiny frame as they return him gently to the shore. Beneath the hands are the root causes of the refugee crisis. War. Ethnic cleansing. Famine. Genocide. Religious persecution. The blood dripping from the fingertips symbolizes the innocent lives lost. The portrait of Aylan's sweet smile is machine quilted. The background is reminiscent of barbed wire. On the back of this quilt, I used car-and-truck-motif fabric that you might find on any young boy's bed quilt. It is important that this baby have a quilt, stitched from *A Mother's Heart*.

Article 14

Carolyn V. Bunkley (Detroit, Michigan), 2016.
50 × 50 inches, commercial and hand-dyed cotton,
cotton batting, monofilament, machine appliquéd.

I believe the word "asylum" means to escape from persecution and to find the freedom to be me, if only in my mind.

My goal was to depict the image of the black man hanging from a telephone pole just as in crucifixion. I used muted denim jeans and dark colors to show the grimness of his plight. The hoodie is made from hand-dyed fabric, and the colors show life fading. Where does the black man go to live without persecution due to his skin color? I hope the viewer will see the isolation, the aloneness, of the black man as he has been targeted like a deer in hunting season. The more we fear him, the more he becomes the one the world despises, so he can never live without persecution. He has been charged with everything that is wrong in society, and carries it on his shoulders as Christ was sacrificed for the sins of the world on his head. Portrayed nightly in the media to condition society to hate and fear him.

Will he have asylum in salvation only?

Where does the black man go for asylum?

Is Anyone Listening to the Conversation?

Deborah Fell (Urbana, Illinois), 2016.
50 × 50 inches, hand-dyed fabric, cotton batting,
photo transfer on cotton, machine pieced and quilted.

Opening a drawer in the bedroom dresser, I grabbed a well-worn but clean T-shirt to wear for the day. Nothing fancy or nothing special, the T-shirt smelled of fresh laundry. Such a simple pleasure in life—to have clean clothes to wear. The refugee crisis in Europe has placed thousands of people in transient lifestyles, living in organized refugee camps and often being homeless. I imagine the impact on clothing—tattered, worn, stained, torn—all evidence of humanity on this blood road. Many refugees have died along the way. Some have drowned in a sea of hope. Some just give up as they face the peril of trying to find a safe place to live; a home country to call their own. And it makes me think of the clothing on their backs, which tells the story of their hardship and heartache.

This quilt's background shows the impact of such circumstances on clothing; it is stained and tattered and has evidence of humanity in its content. There are ghostlike people walking and trying to find safety in a very dangerous world. Some are only fragments of images. Some are children. Many are walking along on the road to find a better life. Many have died along the way. They do not have the simple luxury of clean clothes. The tattered clothing parallels their tattered life.

Is Anyone Listening to the Conversation? is a reminder to be grateful for the simple things in life. Like putting on that clean T-shirt, or having a safe place for our children. Art is a powerful tool that can serve as a stepping stone to awareness of other people's struggles.

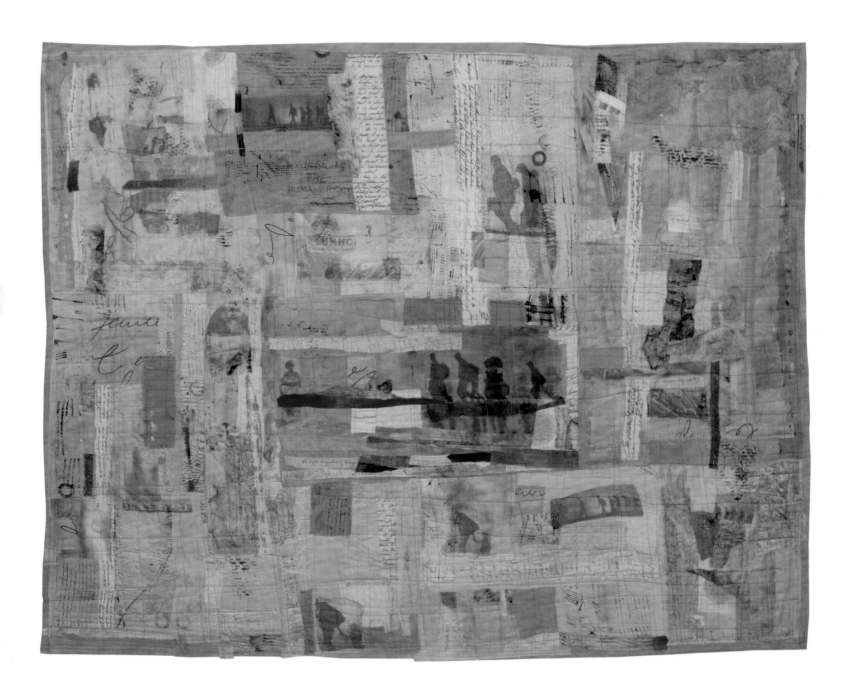

The Children's Exodus: The Walk of the Innocents

Peggie Hartwell (Summerville, South Carolina), 2016.
50 × 50 inches, hand-dyed and commercial cotton, cotton batting, machine appliquéd and quilted.

"A journey of 1,000 miles starts with a single step." —Lao Tzu

And so they gathered onto themselves the courage to release their sons and daughters to walk an unknown "journey" into another world, where hope is possible and peace is probable and hunger and violence would become things of the past. They, the parents, dare to send their children (their dreams, their beloveds) from Central America through Mexico to their destination—America, where their greatest gifts of love would find a better life in their host country. What an undertaking! Faith and hope would truly have embraced them!

And so they gathered upon themselves the courage to leave their parents and their loved ones to walk an unknown "journey" they had only dreamed of. Leaving behind memories as they embraced the hope and walked silently into the darkness, never to look back lest their wills would be broken and the journey would become impossible. They pushed forward; this love that had gathered in their parents' bosom became the strength they would walk upon as they entered into the night searching for the tomorrow of their dreams.

This quilt is dedicated to the countless migrant children who walked across borders from Central America to America for a better life.

Dedicated to the countless mothers who loved them enough to let them go.

99

Home

Renee Allen (Ellenwood, Georgia), 2016.
50 × 50 inches, commercial fabric, hand painting,
cotton batting, machine appliquéd and quilted.

A safe place to live is the foundation for human beings to thrive. This safe place to live, often called home, is a fundamental right of everyone. In almost every culture there is a word for "home"; for example, *huis*, *tehuis*, *abode*, *verblijf*, *lof*, *woning*, or *zij*.

A home will allow individuals to develop healthier biological systems. With a safe place to live, communities can then be established and families flourish. In communities the need for education is often cultivated and amplified. Commerce has an opportunity to develop. In safe places to live, individuals can flourish emotional and physically.

Without a safe shelter, children living in conflict areas are deprived of basic needs such as shelter, food, and medical attention. This deprivation can severely impact their life span. Adolescent soldiers armed with AK-47s are often used as human shields and to clear land mines. These children are subjected to sexual abuse and exploitation. War zones in thirty-six countries have employed children as soldiers.

This human right resonates deeply within me because I enjoy the comfort of my home, to replenish my body, mind, and spirit.

ARTICLE 15.

(1) Everyone has the right to a nationality.
(2) No one shall be arbitrarily deprived of his nationality nor denied the right to change his nationality.

Annie Grey (West Chester, Ohio), 2017.
50 × 50 inches, commercial fabric, printed, cotton batting, machine quilted.

Flags for the Dispossessed

The United Nations Declaration of Human Rights, Article 15, states that all people should have a nationality. People without a nationality are referred to as being stateless and are not recognized as citizens of any country. They have no legal identity and have difficulty securing work, housing, education, and medical care. In addition, they cannot exit and reenter a country freely. Lack of nationality can often be caused by war and conflict, and by laws prohibiting women from conveying nationality to their children upon birth.

Statelessness is a global problem affecting fifteen million people. The status of Dominicans of Haitian descent in the Dominican Republic is an example of a country denying a people's citizenship. This quilt is dedicated to the 200,000 Dominicans of Haitian descent who were stripped of their birthright and citizenship in 2013 by the Dominican Supreme Court in the Dominican Republic. This ruling was found to violate the United Nations Universal Declaration of Human Rights. It is my hope that all the stateless find a country to accept them and call home.

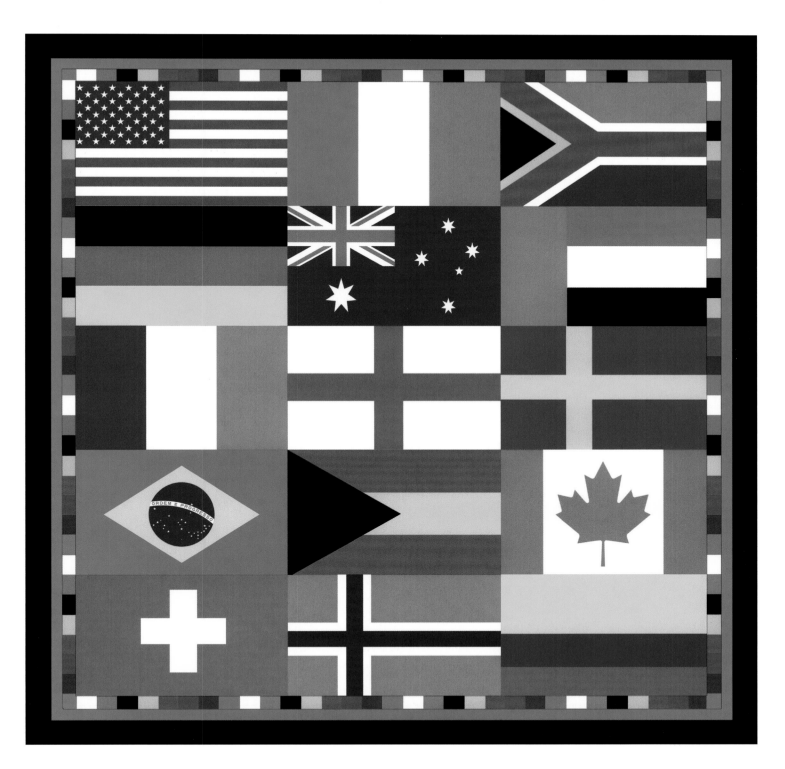

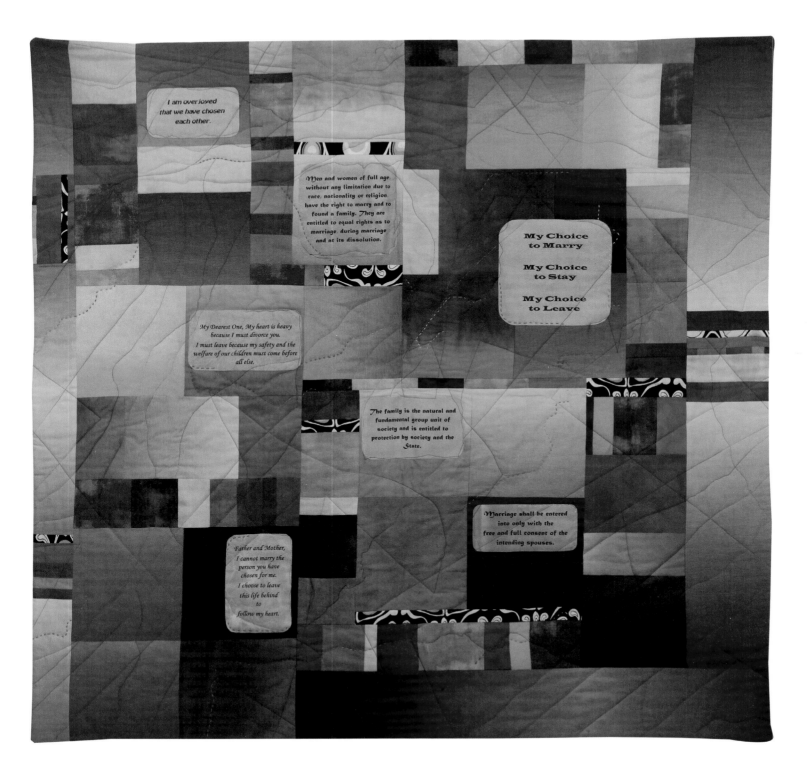

ARTICLE 16.

(1) Men and women of full age, without any limitation due to race, nationality or religion, have the right to marry and to found a family. They are entitled to equal rights as to marriage, during marriage and at its dissolution.
(2) Marriage shall be entered into only with the free and full consent of the intending spouses.
(3) The family is the natural and fundamental group unit of society and is entitled to protection by society and the State.

I Am Overjoyed We Have Chosen Each Other

Carole Lyles Shaw (Bradenton, Florida), 2016.
50 × 50 inches, commercial fabric, photo transfer on cotton, hand painting, cotton batting, machine appliquéd and quilted.

I chose Article 16 because I believe that marriage choice is central to a free and open society for all citizens. The freedom to choose one's spouse is denied to women through tradition, custom, religion, or law in many parts of the world. Therefore, this article is about so much more than marriage equality. It speaks to the freedom of women to live a full and free life on their own terms. Marriage choice is inextricably linked to other rights; for example, the right of young girls to get a secular education and pursue a career outside the home.

This article also speaks to the right of an individual to choose to leave a marriage. I thought about how an individual might reject a forced marriage or initiate a divorce. When I started designing this quilt, I wrote short letters and a poem that I printed on fabric. I wanted to use just a few words that could hint at the strong emotions behind such choices. I also printed the language of the article on fabric.

This is my modem approach to a "story quilt" using an abstract/modem design—asymmetrical, minimalist, improvisational, and employing a rich but limited color palette.

Bliss

Carole Gary Staples (West Chester, Ohio), 2016.
50 × 50 inches, commercial fabric, hand painting, cotton batting, netting, ribbon, lace, beads, silk flowers, photo transfer on cotton, machine appliquéd and quilted.

The Sixteenth Article of the United Nations Human Rights Declaration is about marriage and family. It states that all grown-ups have the right to marry and have a family if they want one, and that men and women have the same rights when they are married and when they are separated.

I view marriage as a relatively simple concept; a union of men and women that is a part of every culture. When I think of marriage, I think of a loving, committed, and consensual relationship. I think of a rite of passage filled with preparation, planning, anticipated joy, and celebration.

Sadly, this is not the case for many around the world. For this reason we must think beyond the bliss, look beyond the obvious, and raise our awareness to understand the importance of this human right. It is speaking to preventing, stopping, and eliminating the atrocities of forced marriages, child marriages, and human trafficking.

On This Our Special Day

Gwendolyn Brooks (Washington, DC), 2016.
50 × 50 inches, commercial fabric, batik, organza,
hand painting on cotton, cotton batting, beads, metallic fabric,
lace, silk flowers, found objects, hand appliquéd and quilted.

Individuals should be free to marry the person they desire regardless race, creed, nationality, or religion. Every human being deserves happiness in sharing their lives with their spouse in peace, joy, and harmony. The viewer of my quilt will observe two young people on their wedding day. This is both a joyous and exciting day for both of them. Notice the beautiful wedding dress that the bride is wearing, complete with diamond earrings. The groom is equally outfitted with a richly textured suit and hat to match. This entire quilt was hand sewn, and the faces of the bride and groom were painted with acrylic paint.

ARTICLE 17.

(1) Everyone has the right to own property alone
as well as in association with others.
(2) No one shall be arbitrarily deprived of his property.

Sharon Ray (Ann Arbor, Michigan), 2016.
50 × 50 inches, commercial fabric, hand painting, photo transfer
on cotton, cotton batting, machine appliquéd and quilted.

Hamtramck, My Home

Growing up in Hamtramck, a town with many people of Polish descent, the powers that be wanted more land to build housing for their children to keep them in the city, with their roots. The City of Hamtramck decided to actively—and by any means necessary—evict the residents of and then tear down homes where a majority of the black population lived.

During this time, a lady was living there with her cancer-stricken elderly mother; the city tried to evict her, but she refused to move. The city cut off her water and refused basic services, like removal of garbage. She still would not move, so the city decided one morning to just tear down the house with them in it. They woke up to the sound of a bulldozer, to which a chain had been attached; the chain was wrapped around the house, and the bulldozer was tearing and pulling at the house. The crew managed to tear down a portion of the house before the daughter ran out, stood in front of the house, and stopped them from further demolition. But they had nowhere to go and had to live in that house the rest of the winter, part of it being exposed to the elements and to the rats that would run in and out.

The lawsuit, *Sarah Garrett v. City of Hamtramck*, is still not totally resolved and is the oldest housing-discrimination lawsuit in the history of this county.

ARTICLE 18.

Everyone has the right to freedom of thought,
conscience and religion; this right includes freedom to change
his religion or belief, and freedom, either alone or in community with
others and in public or private, to manifest his religion or belief
in teaching, practice, worship and observance.

Michelle Flamer (Philadelphia, Pennsylvania), 2016.
50 × 50 inches, commercial fabric, cotton batting, machine
and hand appliquéd and machine quilted.

A Prayer for All Girls

When the Boko Haram kidnapped 276 Nigerian school girls in the middle of the night on April 14, 2014, news of that act of terror spread across the globe. The Twitter hashtag #bringbackourgirls drew the attention of First Lady Michelle Obama and Nobel Peace Prize winner Malala Yousafzai. Malala wrote an open letter to the girls in which she expressed hope that they would be released and able to resume their education, which had been denied by the brutality of their captors. Since 2014 we have learned that the kidnapped girls were forced to renounce their Christian faith and marry their abductors. Some have died, a few have escaped or been released through negotiation, and many have been forced to bear children in captivity.

This quilt is a prayer that all girls will receive the opportunity for a good education and have the right to worship as they please and marry whom they love.

ARTICLE 19.

Everyone has the right to freedom of opinion and expression; this right includes freedom to hold opinions without interference and to seek, receive and impart information and ideas through any media and regardless of frontiers.

Peggie Hartwell (Summerville, South Carolina), 2016. 46 × 47.5 inches, cotton batiks, nylon, cotton threads and batting, machine appliquéd and quilted.

Do You Know Me?

Do you know me? Can you see me? Really see me? I am the dreams of many, the love of most, and the fears of some. I am so loved by my family. They have such high hopes for me! But the hard-paved street has hopes for me also. Hidden before me is a "welcome mat" carved in the pavement, laid out offering me anything and everything; a different kind of life. I need only to "adjust my thoughts, friends, words, and deeds! Can you image that?!!" "No!" I heard my family whisper in my ear. "You cannot have him! We will not let the hard, cold pavement claim him; you will not welcome his steps! He will 'shake the dust' off his feet and step forward, into a world where imagination and dreams will embrace him. Life will be possible because he believes in something more: tomorrow!"

Dedicated to mothers and their sons who survive the streets of today!

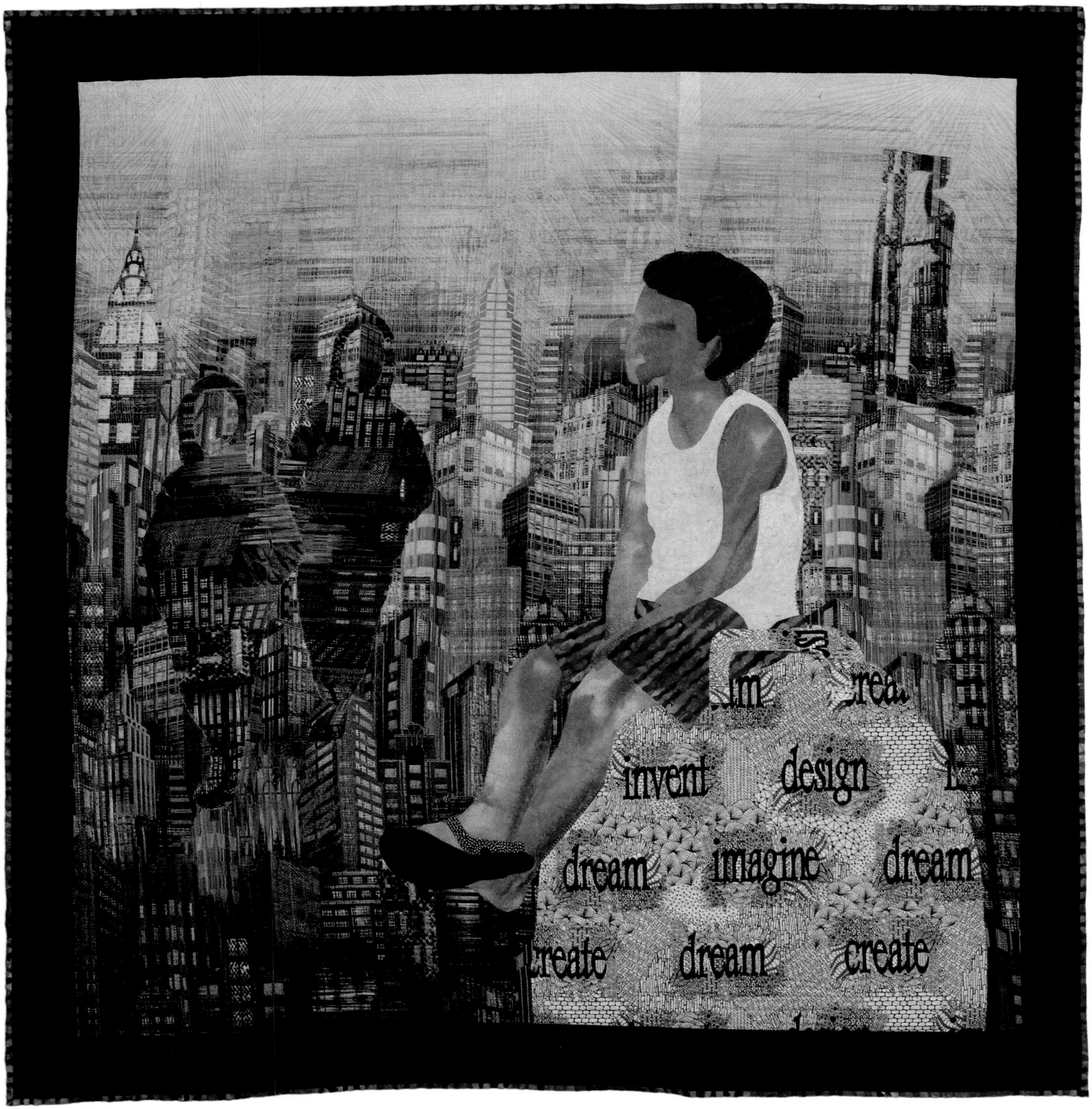
invent
design
dream
imagine
dream
create
dream
create

Dawn Williams Boyd (Atlanta, Georgia), 2016.
50 × 50 inches, commercial fabric, hand painting,
photo transfer on cotton, acrylic paint, cotton batting,
machine appliquéd and quilted.

Freedom of Speech

Hundreds of reporters, journalists, and war correspondents have died just because they were doing their jobs, in the face of inherent danger, in order to bring us stories from around the globe that are critical to our understanding of ourselves and our fellow man. Whether they are embedded in military units, ensconced at city desks, or covering street demonstrations around the world, reporters are subject to blackballing, imprisonment, kidnapping, and murder for the words they write and disseminate. The role of the free press should be that of intermediary between the powerful and the people they govern, not the purveyor of propaganda and lies. When the powers that be are threatened by the truth, the press's access to that power is limited or bypassed altogether. Often, the press is blamed—and punished—for inciting dissatisfaction and revolt.

Suppression of free speech is neither a modern phenomenon nor regulated to war-torn eras. All of known history could be seen as a series of newspaper articles, reported first- or secondhand, in order to let those of us who were not there know what happened. Or could it be only what the powerful want us to know?

The very concept of "freedom of speech" has changed radically since the emergence of the World Wide Web. The preponderance of fake news and misinformation has resulted in the willingness of some zealots to "do something" about situations that don't truly exist. Even more worrisome is the miseducation of our citizens and especially our youth, some of whom will believe anything they read online without the benefit of fact checking or research.

The job of journalists is changing, but their vulnerability to censorship, imprisonment, and physical harm increases with every story.

Freedom of Expression over the Water

Gloria Kellon (Shaker Heights, Ohio), 2016.
50 × 50 inches, commercial fabric, cotton batting,
machine appliquéd and quilted.

Throughout the world, people—both children and adults—have the same basic wants and needs.

Freedom of expression is one of these needs. This quilt uses large extraordinary waves of the oceans and seas of our world to symbolize this concept. All are often haunted by the need to express their emotions, ideas, and talents. These quilt stitches illustrate many of the possibilities of expression flowing across the waters of the world. Freedom of expression should be an entitlement of living. It is as if the soul must be fulfilled, and expression is the vehicle. The drive to write, to lead, to protest, and to create stems from within. Music and art in their many formats stream from a person's inner being, which feeds that soul and the souls of others. The sound of music tames, inspires, and gives enjoyment to us all. Art in any of its many forms can speak the words needed to cause changes, give understanding, and mirror unfathomable beauty or reality. Quilts, with their graphic as well as narrative quality, exemplify this idea. Words that make the great poem or dynamic novel have fulfilled the writer as well as the reader. Expression also comes in the form of leading, acting, or infinite skill in a profession such as medicine, science, mathematics, or education. Through expression, lives are enriched, society is enhanced, and the soul is at peace. Freedom of expression is a right of life.

Freedom of Expression: Human Right #19

Marjorie Freeman (Durham, North Carolina), 2016.
50 × 50 inches, commercial fabric, organza, beads,
buttons, pen and fabric markers, cotton batting, paper piecing,
machine and hand appliquéd and quilted.

I selected Freedom of Expression as the basic human right to present artistically in fabric because that human right has had the greatest impact on my personal life and, in my opinion, holds the key to peace among all people everywhere.

Once my physical needs and security issues are resolved, I find my greatest joy in the arts: reading, writing, listening to music of all types, attending theater and dance performances, visiting art museums, creating art quilts, and interacting with friends, often discussing my experiences. Life is unimaginable if I am not able to express myself and communicate with my family, friends, and those whose opinions are not the same as mine. I cannot live without mental stimulation and interactions as they give more meaning and happiness to my life. This quilt is meant to express that which I enjoy most in life, none of which is done in complete isolation from another person. Some activities may be done alone, but even then, we are sharing the thoughts and ideas and beliefs of others who created the words or work. Everything on this quilt represents a form of self-expression. Even our style of dress expresses something about us. The sign language spelling out "freedom" speaks for those who cannot speak aloud as most of us do. "Love," written in Braille, expresses the desire of the blind to communicate using the written word, as do those blessed with sight.

People have the freedom to express themselves even when we disagree with their ideas, beliefs, thoughts, or opinion. How boring the world would be if all our thoughts and ideas were the same! Our lives are enriched when we take the time to *listen* to others and to truly understand concepts and events from another's perspective. Today's world is shrinking as people gain and share information from every corner of the world, thanks to advances in technology. It is my hope that this quilt stimulates viewers to open their minds and broaden their perspectives, by seeking, receiving, and sharing mentally and verbally with *all* people in every community. Extending this freedom of expression to each person in every state and nation of the world could bring about the peace we all desire, which is truly essential to our very survival on this earth.

ARTICLE 20.

(1) Everyone has the right to freedom of peaceful assembly and association.
(2) No one may be compelled to belong to an association.

Julius Bremer (Cleveland, Ohio), 2016.
50 × 50 inches, commercial fabric, cotton batting, machine appliquéd and quilted.

Let's Gather Peacefully

One of the most basic rights of the human race is that we are allowed, as well as expected to be able, to assemble. To be able to peacefully assemble, be it in our churches, supermarkets, schools, political houses, sports arenas, or anywhere else, is the foundation for the advancement of intelligent discourse throughout the human race.

Humans will grow only when we can share our differences, scientific knowledge, educational techniques, and many other advances. If we cannot find peaceful grounds to assemble, humankind will atrophy and become as primal as the lowest form of life on the planet.

Humankind must flourish and continue to move forward toward a unified race, and to do so, we must be able to share this world in a peaceful manner.

Magical Dreaming of the Right to Public Assembly

Adrienne Cruz (Portland, Oregon), 2017.
50 × 50 inches, hand-dyed cotton, cotton batting, commercial cotton, pieced, and machine quilted.

Stand Together, Stand Alone

However we choose in Righteousness and Grace
Gathering, collaborating, expressing

Being who we are

Respectfully

As stars of our galaxy, our universe Reflecting, giving,
receiving, being Our unique individual selves

In light of day and dark of night

Standing on the shoulders of those who came before us
Speaking our truth

Witnessing change

Creating avenues for Peace and Understanding
Stand Together, Stand Alone

However we choose

To respectfully be who we are.

ARTICLE 21.

(1) Everyone has the right to take part in the government of his country, directly or through freely chosen representatives.
(2) Everyone has the right of equal access to public service in his country.
(3) The will of the people shall be the basis of the authority of government; this will shall be expressed in periodic and genuine elections which shall be by universal and equal suffrage and shall be held by secret vote or by equivalent free voting procedures.

Deeds, Not Words

Carolyn Crump (Houston, Texas), 2016.
50 × 50 inches, commercial fabric, cotton batting, machine appliquéd and quilted.

Article 21 of the UN Declaration of Human Rights states that all individuals should be able to vote. In my quilt, *Deeds, Not Words*, I chose to visualize the difficulty women had to endure to get the right to vote. Women were very restricted as to what they could or couldn't do, whether it be at work, at home, or in the community. Women had no input in issues such as divorce rights, access to education, owning property, or better working conditions. Women wanted the vote to secure power in the societies where they lived, and over their lives. Women did not have the basic human right of having the privilege to vote. Voting was a way to participate in how the national, state, and local government is run. There were movements in many countries by women to get the right to vote. At the time, most countries around the world were run by men.

The slogan "Deeds, Not Words" was coined by English suffragette Emmeline Pankhurst (1858–1928), of the Women's Social and Political Union in England, founded in 1903. The aim of the organization was to secure women the right to vote. In the quilt, I illustrate an incident in England where a suffragette, Emily Davison, was knocked down by a horse at Epsom Derby as she stepped onto the racetrack. She tried to disrupt the race to draw attention to the suffragettes' cause. Davison, a militant campaigner for women's right to vote, died of her injuries four days later.

The Nineteenth Amendment to the US Constitution granted women the right to vote in 1920. It took women in the United States seventy years of protesting to get this right.

Lift Every Voice

Charlotte Hunter (Cincinnati, Ohio), 2016.
50 × 50 inches, commercial fabric, ribbon, beads,
buttons, found objects, photo transfer on cotton,
cotton batting, machine appliquéd and quilted.

In April 1994 the first free and fair democratic election was held in South Africa. Citizens of all races participated, signaling the first election there with universal adult suffrage. The election was overseen by the Independent Electoral Commission, formed to assure a fair election process after the end of apartheid.

On the basis of his civil rights expertise, a Cincinnatian, Judge Nathaniel Jones, participated in the trials to end apartheid. He also assisted in the negotiations to establish a fair democratic voting process.

Similarly, when African Americans truly exercised their right to vote, the first African American president, Barack Obama, was elected.

Therefore, this quilt reflects two freedom songs: "We Shall Overcome" by Cincinnatian Louise Shropshire, and the national anthem of South Africa, "Nkosi Sikelel'i Afrika," composed by Enoch Sontonga, a Xhosa clergyman at a Methodist mission.

This quilt reflects the National Underground Railroad Freedom Center's mission to recognize freedom fighters around the world.

Recognizing South Africa's transition from apartheid to democracy, three key figures received the National Underground Railroad Freedom Conductor Award: Archbishop Desmond Tutu, 2000; Nelson Mandela, 2014; and Judge Nathaniel Jones, 2016.

ARTICLE 22.

Everyone, as a member of society, has the right to social security and is entitled to realization, through national effort and international co-operation and in accordance with the organization and resources of each State, of the economic, social and cultural rights indispensable for his dignity and the free development of his personality.

Dorothy Burge (Chicago, Illinois), 2016.
50 × 50 inches, hand-dyed commercial cotton, cotton batting, photo transfer on cotton, machine appliquéd, pieced, and quilted.

Stop Killing Us

"Stop Killing Us" became the rallying cry for African Americans whose lives were threatened by police, community, and family violence. This quilt is one of the ways that I stand up against this assault and add my voice to this movement. It is my way to give a face to the many young people who have been killed or traumatized by violence. As a mother, my heart breaks every time I hear the story of another young person who has been killed. Article 22 of the Universal Declaration of Human Rights, the right to social security, states, "The society you live in should provide you with social security and the rights necessary for your dignity and development." The "Stop Killing Us" movement is not a call for sympathy. It is a call for the lives of African American youth to be respected, valued, and protected.

Wealth of the World

Trish Williams (Peoria, Illinois) and
Dorothy Burge (Chicago, Illinois), 2016.
50 × 50 inches, hand-dyed commercial cotton,
wire mesh, photo transfer on cotton, cotton batting,
machine piecing, and quilted.

When I started this quilt I spent hours doing research to see what I could find, and that turned out to be a labor of love. I used several websites that supplied this type of data to compile my list. Canada is the leading country in the field of medicine or pharmaceuticals. France is the leader in medical help for those who are ill and for the aged. Japan is the leader in childcare. Qatar is a wealthy nation, and income is not an issue for its population. South Korea is the leader in education. The United States has the most affordable housing plan. Since then, some of these results may have changed. Every nation's citizens should be able to benefit from the wealth of their country.

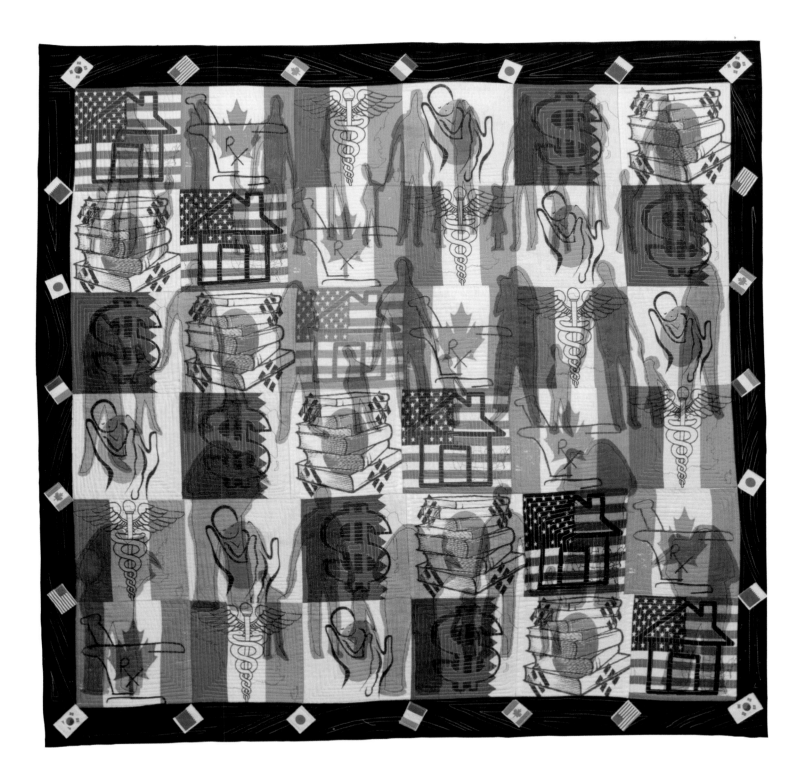

Art and Healing

Ed Johnetta Miller (Hartford, Connecticut), 2016.
50 × 50 inches, commercial cotton, photo transfer,
cotton batting, machine pieced, appliquéd, and quilted.

I first became aware of how devastating malaria was for people as a design consultant for Aid to Artisans in Ghana.

Working in the villages outside Kumasi, in hot rainy weather, I watched puddles of standing water. Hundreds of mosquitoes landed and bred in these puddles—as well as in cups, containers, or anything else that held water—and came out at night to bite people. Within a week of my arrival, several of the artists in my workshop had come down with cases of malaria. This was overwhelming for me. I had the proper medication to help prevent malaria, and also had a treated net to sleep under at night, but the majority of Ghanaian people I worked with had no such relief. I felt compelled to do something about this in whatever way I could.

In a talk I gave at a local school in Connecticut, I spoke about my travels, and how malaria is the leading killer of children and adults in many African countries, despite there being many ways to prevent it. In the audience was a dentist who had just returned from the Ivory Coast, and she asked if we could sit and talk. Dr. Decker told me about the "Nothing but Nets—Send a Net, Save a Life" program that was coming to her daughter's school, and she asked if I would like to work with them on a project pertaining to malaria prevention.

From then, I developed a workshop called "Anyone Can Create Art for Nets" where I go into schools and talk about malaria and teach collage, making note cards, quilting, and jewelry designing. We sell these items at special school events to raise money to purchase treated nets for families to sleep under, and we have been able to send hundreds of nets to sub-Saharan Africa. We are having very successful workshops, and I hope to continue to be a champion for "Nothing but Nets."

ARTICLE 23.

(1) Everyone has the right to work, to free choice of employment, to just and favorable conditions of work and to protection against unemployment.
(2) Everyone, without any discrimination, has the right to equal pay for equal work.
(3) Everyone who works has the right to just and favorable remuneration ensuring for himself and his family an existence worthy of human dignity, and supplemented, if necessary, by other means of social protection.
(4) Everyone has the right to form and to join trade unions for the protection of his interests.

Sylvia Hernandez (Brooklyn, New York), 2016.
50 × 50 inches, commercial cotton, cotton batting, machine appliquéd and quilted.

Right to Work

This quilt is a celebration of female labor leaders. Pauline Newman was a factory worker, teacher, and labor rights activist. Mother Jones was a teacher, dressmaker, community organizer, and organized labor representative. Dolores Huerta is a teacher, labor leader, and civil rights activist. I recommend you take some time and read up on these women.

The woman in the center of the quilt is Melanie Soto Gonzalez; she is a structural engineer and I celebrate her because she is my parents' granddaughter. My father would have been beside himself with her. This photo of her was taken on a bridge she helped build in Morocco. Melanie Soto Gonzalez is the product of the work done by Dolores, Mother Jones, and Pauline.

RIGHT TO WORK, EVERYONE HAS THE RIGHT TO FREE CHOICE OF EMPLOYMENT, TO JUST AND FAVOURABLE CONDITIONS OF WORK. WITHOUT ANY DISCRIMINATION, THE RIGHT TO EQUAL PAY FOR EQUAL WORK.

23

A Woman's Worth: Equal Pay for Equal Work

Earamichia Brown (New York, New York), 2017.
36 × 48 inches, commercial cotton, cotton batting, silk and leather
fabrics and Mistyfuse, fused, machine appliquéd and quilted.
Images of women on currency used with permission from AAUW.org.

On March 27, 2017, Trump revoked the 2014 Fair Pay and Safe Workplaces order, which then president Barack Obama put in place to ensure that companies with federal contracts comply with fourteen labor and civil rights laws. In an attempt to keep the worst violators from receiving taxpayer dollars, the Fair Pay order included two rules that affected women workers: paycheck transparency and a ban on forced arbitration clauses for sexual harassment, sexual assault, or discrimination claims.

This piece is specific to the gender pay gap. There are two distinct numbers regarding the pay gap: unadjusted versus adjusted pay gap, the latter of which takes into account differences in hours worked, occupations chosen, education, and job experience. For example, someone who takes time off (e.g., maternity leave) will likely not earn as much as someone who does not take time off from work. Factors like this contribute to lower yearly earnings for women, but when all external factors have been adjusted for, there still exists a gender pay gap in many situations (between 4.8% and 7.1% according to one study). Unadjusted pay gaps are much higher. In the United States, for example, the unadjusted average female's annual salary has commonly been cited as being 78 percent of the average male salary.

The American Association of University Woman created the images that are incorporated in this piece. I have obtained permission to use them. These bills are a visual representation of the inequality that exists in the workforce. This is our America, and America is governed by an administration that does not support women's rights.

The woman in this picture graduated from Harvard University and Georgetown Law School, and she still makes less than most white men in similar positions. Many women are highly credentialed and will make less than their lesser-credentialed male counterparts. This is the reality of the American job force. We demand *Equal Pay for Equal Work*.

ARTICLE 24.

Everyone has the right to rest and leisure, including reasonable limitation of working hours and periodic holidays with pay.

No Rest for the Weary

Sauda Zahra (Durham, North Carolina), 2016.
50 × 50 inches, hand-dyed and commercial cotton, cotton batting, machine appliquéd and quilted.

According to the Human Rights Watch organization, there are millions of people, the majority women and girls, who work as domestics in private households around the world. Domestic workers globally share a common history of having to work long hours for low wages, and often in inhumane work environments. These circumstances prevent domestic workers from having the freedom to determine how their time is spent, and as a consequence, many domestic workers can only imagine what it would be like to have "free" time to rest from work and relax.

No Rest for the Weary is a visual interpretation of the realities of being a domestic worker. The quilt highlights domestic workers performing common household tasks in different parts of the world, as illustrated by the map fabric featured prominently in the attic window quilt block pattern. Symbols of time are used throughout the quilt to reinforce how much control employers have over domestic workers' time, and how illusive time can seem to domestic workers who have

little control over when and how they use their time to rest from work and relax.

Domestic workers have banned together by forming local, national, and international organizations to raise awareness of their working conditions and demand equal treatment in the workforce. These empowered domestic workers are celebrated in the quilt with the image of a worker dressed in a traditional domestic uniform. As she raises a tool of her profession in protest, declaring that domestic workers' rights are human rights, she is also envisioning the day when all domestic workers will have the "free" time they deserve to rest from work and relax at the beach, a universal example of leisure.

No Rest for the Weary organically evolved into a U-shaped design, further illuminating domestic workers as a united group with pride in their profession, a determination to improve the quality of their lives, and a passion to make the human right to rest from work and relax a reality for all domestic workers around the world.

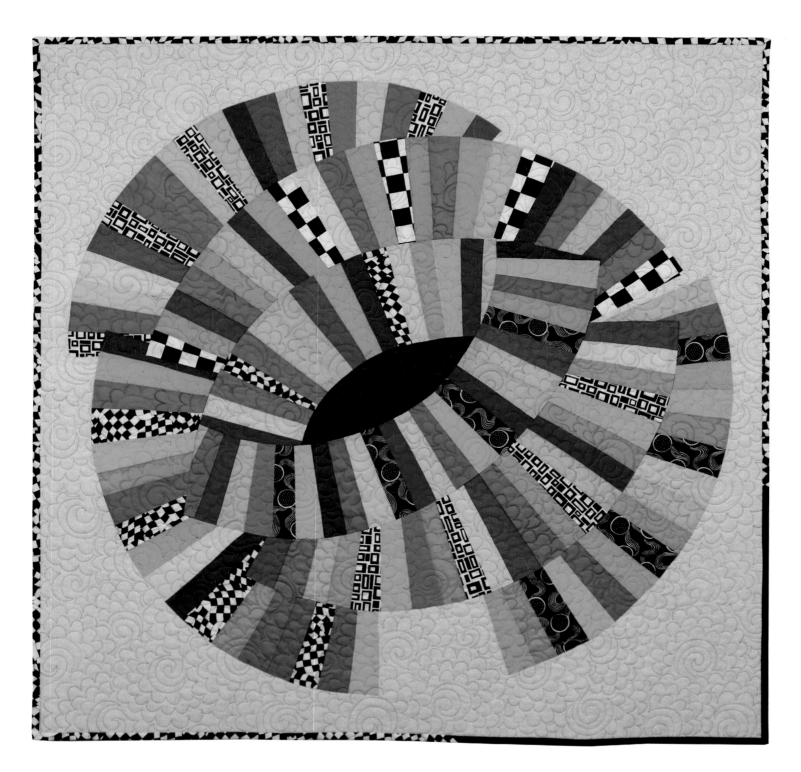

To Go Play in the Sun

Angie Turner (St. Louis, Missouri), 2017.
50 × 50 inches, commercial cotton, cotton batting,
pieced, appliquéd, machine quilted.

To "play" is a forgotten need and, in many cases, an ignored right. Play is the ability to let go of responsibilities and just be yourself. Many of us take the idea of play for granted. Some consider play only for children, but I argue this is not true. The dictionary describes "play" as something fun and amusing, like a game or sport. Yet, I reason that play is simply a respite from work. Work is about taking care of business. Play is about taking care of yourself.

The wealthy have more resources; therefore they have more time to spend at play and tend to take "play" for granted. On the contrary, the less money you have, the less time you have to play. The working class must schedule time, save up money, and work jobs in between to take advantage of "play."

In my art quilt, black represents work, and the arcs of color represent our escape from work. Yellow represents the sunshine and all the wonders of the world. We all have the right to play, rest, and just be, for no other reason except that we are worthy.

ARTICLE 25.

(1) Everyone has the right to a standard of living adequate for the health and well-being of himself and of his family, including food, clothing, housing and medical care and necessary social services, and the right to security in the event of unemployment, sickness, disability, widowhood, old age or other lack of livelihood in circumstances beyond his control.
(2) Motherhood and childhood are entitled to special care and assistance. All children, whether born in or out of wedlock, shall enjoy the same social protection.

Harbor View Encampment

Cynthia Catlin (San Pedro, California), 2016.
50 × 50 inches, hand-dyed and commercial cotton, cotton batting, machine appliquéd and quilted.

Since the beginning of humanity, individuals have experienced a basic human need for food and shelter. Yet, we witness growing homeless communities all over the United States. In my city there is a huge dichotomy of beauty and poverty. We have lawyers and other professionals in their high-rise office building right next to a homeless encampment, both overlooking the breathtaking ocean view and cruise ship excursions. As more people became homeless, the tiny house project was born. In an effort to address the homeless population, a four-by-six-foot, one-room wooden structure on wheels was built. It is meant to replace a tent; however, many cities refuse to allow them to be parked on the public streets. Although they provide basic shelter against the elements and are safer than sleeping on the sidewalks, they are not a viable solution for the homeless crisis. As we continue to study and debate the challenge of homelessness with compassion and diligence, homeless encampments are becoming permanent fixtures. It is a complicated subject with many causes, and the prescription has many layers. We must defend our basic human right for affordable housing and must work to rectify this crisis. On the journey to bring about change, we must realign and reexamine our values for all humans and embrace the task to end homelessness; only then can we all prosper.

Article 25

Glenda Richardson (Ft. Washington, Maryland), 2016.
50 × 50 inches, hand-dyed and commercial cotton, photo
transfer, cotton batting, machine appliquéd and quilted.

Article 25 speaks to the right of everyone to a basic standard of living and social services to support an individual's health and well-being. It seeks to protect those who are sick, disabled, widowed, unemployed, or aged. I set out the tenets of the article in bold type. I was particularly struck by the fact that the mother and child were singled out for special consideration, the child representing the most vulnerable among us. Due to gender bias, women are often subjected to domestic violence, lack of maternal care, sex trafficking, and lack of educational opportunities. This breeds the conditions that require the services outlined in Article 25. When a mother is affected, a generation of children are affected as well. I strive for my work to have an emotional impact on the viewer. In this piece I focused on the vulnerability of the child and the protective stance of the mother.

A Crying Shame

Linda Ali (Novi, Michigan), 2016.
50 × 50 inches, commercial cotton, cotton blend, polyester, beads, acrylic yarn, hand appliquéd, hand embroidered, hand beaded, and machine quilted.

The greatest asset of any country or culture is its children. Therefore, to nurture, protect, and provide for their physical and mental well-being is paramount. Naturally, this responsibility rests primarily with parent(s) or caregivers or both. Unfortunately, there are frequent reports (from around the world) that children are being subjected to unspeakable acts of violence that threatens not only their healthy growth and development, but their very lives. Regardless of whether children live in the most-affluent communities or countries, or the most poverty stricken, no area, it seems, is exempt from these acts. They occur without regard to ethnicity, gender, or social or economic status. The effects can be tantamount to a debilitating disease.

Violence against children takes many different forms. Sadly, many instances of violence perpetrated against children are committed by those entrusted with their care.

There are numerous and frequent reports related to the effects of violence against children. For instance, it is commonly shown that children who are repeatedly victimized are at greater risk of repeating those acts as an adult.

Studies have also shown that children subjected to violence are also

more prone to juvenile delinquency,
more susceptible to drug and alcohol abuse,
more likely to be a school dropout,
more likely to live in poverty,
more likely to have poor health, and
more likely to die young.

We cannot close our eyes or turn a deaf ear to this problem.

Thirty-five years of my professional life were spent as a pediatric nurse practitioner advocating for the health and well-being of children and families. During those years, too often I witnessed the damage to steadily increasing numbers of children caused by violence in all of its ugly forms. Reliable, accessible resources were not always available. Fortunately, however, the United Nations member states have recognized the urgent need to address this problem and have formed a global partnership that is committed to ending all forms of violence against children by the year 2030.

150

Without Consent: Afterward

Linda Ali (Novi, Michigan), 2016.
50 × 50 inches, commercial cotton, yarn, crystals,
buttons, cotton batting, machine appliquéd and quilted.

On October 4, 1951, Henrietta Lacks died from metastatic cervical cancer and its complications at Johns Hopkins Hospital in Baltimore, Maryland.

No one would have predicted that this young, thirty-one-year-old African American wife and mother, a mere five feet two inches tall, would be responsible for the world's first line of laboratory-grown human cells that remained alive. Today, these cells have been instrumental in worldwide biological research and development.

The cervical tumors removed from Mrs. Lacks and saved for scientific use were taken not only without consent, but against the specific wishes of her husband.

When the scientific community determined that these cells (known as "He La cells") did not die, as others had been known to, but continued to multiply, researchers mailed or handed vials of the cells to other researchers and scientists all around the world. The cells were used in experiments at either no cost or for a meager twenty-five dollars.

Obtained without consent and against the wishes of a woman and her family, these cells led not only to great medical and scientific advances, but to changes in the laws and ethics related to medical care in the country and around the world.

Living in the Shadows

Marion Coleman (Castro Valley, California), 2016.
50 × 50 inches, commercial cotton, cotton batting,
machine appliquéd and quilted.

From the moment of their birth until their very last breath, some people will never experience the human rights presented in Article 25 in the Universal Declaration of Human Rights. Although Article 25 states that everyone has the right to an adequate standard of living and well-being, including security during unemployment, sickness, disability, widowhood, old age, or other lack of livelihood, because of circumstances beyond our control so many of us will not experience these rights. Even more discouraging is the particular risk to mothers and children who are entitled to special care and assistance.

There are many reasons for violations to these rights, which may include poverty, discrimination, intolerance, isolation, social and political unrest, substance abuse, and lack of education and opportunity, along with location of birth, to name a few.

Living in the Shadows provides a glimpse of worldwide conditions related to violations of these rights. Citizens around the globe suffer a shadow life where they are seen but unseen. There are mothers who may have had children without the benefit of marriage and its protections. Often these women have not received an adequate education and therefore cannot take advantage of the opportunities that such an education provides. This of course makes them subject to low-wage jobs or significant unemployment. So the primary figures in the piece are designed to show a mother's love while being surrounded by the shadows of the unobtainable.

The children sitting and eating addresses the crisis for children who are affected by poverty, hunger, wars, social unrest, and disease. These children may be fleeing wars and sometimes traveling great distances alone. There are orphans left to provide for themselves because all of their family members have died from Ebola or AIDS. Then there are children in more-developed nations whose parents are under- or unemployed and cannot afford adequate food or housing.

The line of men is designed to show the volume of individuals living in homeless encampments, in temporary shelters, or on the streets. There are also those who have lost jobs and cannot afford to stay in their homes and may live in cars or motels or sleep on the sofa of a friend or family member. This presents long-term individual and community inadequacies related to discrimination, substance abuse, mental illness, war, unemployment, isolation, and the dismantling of social systems.

The solitary female figure shows that as the poor and disenfranchised get old, their medical conditions persist. Isolation and danger surround them and become different but equally menacing shadows.

Living in the Shadows is ultimately a visual examination of how precarious life can be. Circumstances such as place of birth, being female, belonging to a certain racial or ethnic group, having a mental or physical illness, or any of life's unexpected events could have any of us living in the shadows.

Share

Selena A. Sullivan (Mint Hill, North Carolina), 2016.
50 × 50 inches; commercial cotton, wool, synthetic fabrics,
cotton batting; hand appliquéd using cotton, wool, and synthetic fabrics;
hand and machine quilted.

I selected Human Rights Article 25 because it took me back to my childhood in the agricultural area of eastern North Carolina, where obtaining the essentials of life was endless work and a constant struggle. My parents were sharecroppers, which required each family member to take an active part in the planting, tending, and harvesting of the crops (corn, cotton, tobacco) that we were required to produce annually for the landowner. Housing was barely basic at best, as the wooden structure we called home contained only a wood-burning stove, no electricity, and no indoor plumbing. The agricultural needs of the landowner had precedence over school attendance and the raising of all the food my family would consume during the year.

The experiences of my youth strengthened me, led me to earn degrees in nutrition and dietetics, made me into the person I am today, and inspired me to create this art quilt expressing the basic needs of all people everywhere.

Human needs for food, shelter, clean water, and healthcare are the same around the world regardless of one's age or economic status or health. At first glance, those who view my quilt see a bounty of food and a scale showing the disproportionate distribution of the world's wealth. Though disparity exists in America, it is very evident in developing countries and in those affected by political unrest, war, natural disasters, and extreme weather events. All these conditions result in massive destruction and often lead to displacement, homelessness, and food shortages. In many countries, "safety nets" do not exist and the populations most affected are the most vulnerable and at the highest risk: mothers, infants, young children, the homeless, and the aged. In addition, the impact of global warming, global food needs and availability, and access to good healthcare cannot be overlooked.

Thirty-plus years working as a registered dietitian and nutritionist have made me keenly aware of every human's need for and right to good food, clean water, decent housing, and adequate healthcare. We can ensure that this reasonable expectation is met when we share the earth's resources equitably and strive for the peaceful coexistence of all people the world over.

Park Bench Rescue

Valerie White (Denver, Colorado), 2016.
50 × 50 inches, commercial and hand-dyed cotton, acrylic paint, cotton batting, hand painting, machine appliquéd and quilted.

I created *Park Bench Rescue* to draw attention to the increasing number of homeless "women" in the United States. There are more than 565,000 women, men, and children in America who are homeless. Even more shameful, the United States has the largest number of homeless women and children among industrialized nations. Not since the Great Depression have so many families been without homes.

We can all learn, act, and share. Learn about ways to end the homeless in your community; act by volunteering at a food bank or by tutoring a child. Last, share by joining local churches and civic organizations that organize clothing drives. Rather than keep a warm coat in your closet, give it to a person in need.

Park Bench Rescue means to SAVE—why not reach out to a homeless person with a simple hello and smile. That would be the simplest and easiest act of kindness.

25th Declaration of
Human Rights
Food and Shelter for
ALL We all have the right
to a good life.. Mothers and
children, people who are old,
unemployed or disabled and all people
have the right to be cared for.

ARTICLE 26.

(1) Everyone has the right to education. Education shall be free, at least in the elementary and fundamental stages. Elementary education shall be compulsory. Technical and professional education shall be made generally available and higher education shall be equally accessible to all on the basis of merit.
(2) Education shall be directed to the full development of the human personality and to the strengthening of respect for human rights and fundamental freedoms. It shall promote understanding, tolerance and friendship among all nations, racial or religious groups, and shall further the activities of the United Nations for the maintenance of peace.
(3) Parents have a prior right to choose the kind of education that shall be given to their children.

Each One Will Teach Two

Dindga McCannon (Philadelphia, Pennsylvania), 2016.
50 × 50 inches; commercial cotton, felt, beads, acrylic paint, yarn; machine appliquéd, pieced, and quilted.

I choose Article 26, the right to education, because I had found out that there are 781 million illiterate adults in the world! Shocking! Of these, 496 million illiterates are women. Almost two-thirds! Unbelievable! One would think that in the United States, with our free public schools, and known as "a Nation of Wealth," that the stats would be better. They are not. Thirty-two million people in the United States can't read. That's 14 percent of the entire population. Inexcusable! Back in the sixties, we used to say "each one, teach one." Nowadays, I say, "each one, teach two," and perhaps we could cause these unacceptable numbers to go down.

Plant a Seed

Beverly Y. Smith (Charlotte, North Carolina), 2016.
50 × 50 inches, commercial cotton, acrylic paint, cotton batting, hand painting, machine embroidery, appliquéd and quilted.

"If you think in terms of a year, plant a seed; if in terms of ten years, plant trees; in terms of 100 years, teach the people." —Confucius

I feel that this quote will ring true a millennium from now. Being a lifelong educator, I have personally experienced the need to continue the fight for gender equality in education. My family has always highly valued education. Coming from a family of five girls, my parents worked several jobs to ensure that we had an opportunity to go to college.

My own experiences and other women who had an impact on education inspired this quilt's message, the message being how important it is to ensure that girls and women around the world have the same chances to receive an education as boys and men.

According to the United Nations Universal Declaration of Human Rights, Article 26 (1949), everyone has the right to an education. It further states education shall be directed to the full development of the human personality and to the strengthening of respect for human rights and fundamental freedoms.

Education is a human right. Studies have showed that girls' education is an investment that brings a wide range of benefits for the girls themselves, their children, and their communities, as well as society as a whole. Unfortunately, millions of girls around the world are still being denied an equitable and good-quality education.

Many issues have a serious impact on educational outcomes locally and around the world. During the nineteenth century, most southern states passed laws prohibiting the education of African Americans, whether slave or free. Prudence Crandall (1803–1890) was a remarkable woman despite the ridicule and harassment she faced fighting for access for equal education. She opened one of the first schools for African American girls in 1832. More recently, the mass kidnapping of over 200 schoolgirls from the Nigerian town of Chibokthe created global outrage, while Malala Yousafzai, who courageously spoke out that girls be allowed to receive an education, was violently attacked because of her views. Both incidents sparked awareness in people to become involved in seeking equality for the education of girls. The secretary general of the United Nations stated that "Malala is a Woman of the Year because . . . by targeting her, extremists showed what they feared most: a girl with a book."

Some remarkable progress has been made toward achieving gender equality in education. Over the past three decades the ratio of girls to boys enrolled in school has risen at all levels. Through my artwork, I envision my legacy will be to share with society the knowledge that education provides opportunities and benefits everyone when women have equal access to a good-quality education.

Malala

Hilda Vest (Detroit, Michigan), 2016.
50 × 50 inches, commercial cotton, yarn, buttons,
cotton batting, machine appliquéd and quilted.

Malala Yousafzai is a symbol of peaceful protest, and at age seventeen she was the youngest person to receive the Nobel Peace Prize. Her journey began when a group of violent fighters, known as the Taliban, invaded Swat Valley, a section of Mingora, the town in Pakistan that was her home. Due to strict religious rulings, girls were ordered to drop out of school and remain at home, while boys were allowed to continue in school. Some obeyed, but not Malala, who not only continued her education but also began to speak out against this unjust ruling through public speeches, TV appearances, and diaries that were sent to the British Broadcasting Corporation (BBC). These diaries were published online as blogs. The Taliban were so incensed by these actions that they cornered her on her school bus and shot her in the head. Her peaceful movement for girls' rights to education and her miraculous recovery brought attention to her plight, thus sparking international efforts for her to receive the prestigious Nobel Peace Prize. Girls were finally allowed to return to school, and Malala remains a symbol of peace, propelled by the nonviolent movement of Dr. Martin Luther King.

The dominant fabric features letters from the language that was Malala's weapon to communicate her message. In contrast, the gun is a reminder of terror and destruction. The headdress, which is known as "hijab," and her garment reflect her pride in being a Muslim. "One child, one teacher can change the world" is one of her famous quotes. Finally, the repetition of circles was inspired by the fact that in biology, circles represent the female gender.

Imagine a World

Nancy Cash (Durham, North Carolina), 2017.
50 × 50 inches, commercial cotton, acrylic paint, dyed cotton, cotton batting, machine piecing and appliquéd, printing on cotton, painting on cotton, embroidery, machine quilted.

Imagine a world where every man, woman, and child is provided the human right to education. Where there is a realization that the benefits of education outweigh the cost of not educating.

Imagine a world where cancer has not killed your mother, father, or friend or has not afflicted your brother, sister, or yourself. Imagine that the person who found the cure is from the country or neighborhood that was once poor with starvation but is now brimming with education.

Imagine a world where there are no records of deaths due to AIDS or epidemics in even the poorest countries because there are no poor countries, since education has provided them the means of self-sufficiency as well as international connections, and they too are sharing in the global economy.

Imagine a world where more is spent on education than on war. Where slogans of world peace have become actions allowing all human beings to enjoy freedom from fear. No fear, no war, no more!

Imagine a world where the money currently spent on prisons is spent on education, because education is providing those most likely to be of the race, class, or religion that makes them targets for prisons a means to support themselves that doesn't involve drugs, guns, and death.

Imagine a world where countries that pride themselves on being leaders of the "free world" no longer have to hide their shame of having homeless men, women, and children, because they have provided education instead of justification for attitudes of bigotry and racism.

Imagine a world where all people have clean water, nutritional food, and sustainable energy capable of serving the needs of the present without compromising the environment for future generations.

Imagine a world where poverty and starvation are words retired from "what used to be" and are never again needed to describe current conditions anywhere in the world.

Imagine a world where economic equality has become a viable alternative to political and philosophical arguments that lack actions needed to provide equality in education. Where dictators and the top one percent are no longer afraid that an educated population will now have clarity and rid the world of disparity.

Imagine in your lifetime that every person, in every country, on every continent, can say, "we educate the world."

My art quilt speaks to the benefits of education by appealing to our desire to resolve the top issues of the world. I chose not to use the image of a known scholar, celebrity, or activist. I chose an imaginary woman because in some areas of the world, females are denied their human right of education. This basic right is for everyone, as represented in the words of the stars.

The circles on the left represent rays of hope for the accomplishment of this goal. Although many world leaders recognize the human right to education, there are still barriers—barriers and prejudices that I believe are rooted in the social norms of political greed and cultural narcissism.

One of my trademarks is to stitch words and expressions into the background of my quilts. The words represent my thoughts and purpose as I create. Sometimes I use contrasting thread to make the words stand out. Often, I blend them into the fabric color, making them my silent partners. In this quilt, I stitched the word "human" on the hand. Other words are stitched in the universe of the background and the sun rays.

The Georgia Colored Industrial School and Home. The School was run by Mrs. Frances Bridges and her husband Benjamin along with three instructors.

Z. Seminary. While studying Jeremiah meets and later marries Arvisena Center a young bright student at Spelman Seminary. Their daughter Zetta attended

educated son. Their son Jeremiah was born in 1865 the same year slavery was abolished. Jeremiah studied to be a minister and carpenter at Atlanta Baptist

Daniel Bridges was born in Georgia in 1808 the same year the slave trade was abolished in the United States. By the 1870's Daniel taught himself to read and write and he and his wife Elvira Volmer

Learning Always Instilled Freedom

Wendell Brown (Columbia, South Carolina), 2017.
50 × 50 inches, commercial cotton, acrylic paint, hand painted, cotton batting, machine appliquéd and quilted.

My great-great-grandfather Daniel Pruitt was born in Lithonia, Georgia, in 1808, the same year the slave trade was abolished in the United States. Though learning to write was illegal for blacks, reading was not illegal for them in America until around the 1830s; however, by the 1870s Daniel had learned to read and write and farmed land that he and his wife, my great-great-grandmother Elvira, owned. Daniel and Elvira had six children and stressed to them the importance of reading, writing, and learning. The middle child, Jeremiah, my great-grandfather, was born in Lithonia only a few years before the Civil War, which abolished slavery.

Jeremiah was educated at Atlanta Baptist Seminary, where he studied to be a minister and a carpenter. When I was growing up, one of Jeremiah's handmade carved carpentry tools hung on a wall in our home.

While at Atlanta Baptist Seminary, Jeremiah met Georgia Center, a student in the second graduating class at Spelman Seminary. At Spelman, Georgia was an involved student who often called on her good friend Jeremiah to help her make such things as signs and holiday ornaments for various school events. Jeremiah and Georgia married in 1894, built a home, and had five children. Georgia died giving birth to a sixth child, who also died.

Jeremiah's parents, David and Elvira, and Georgia's parents, Jacob and Arsvisena, both stressed the importance of education. Understanding the importance of learning, after the death of his wife, Georgia, Jeremiah sent his young daughter Zetta, my grandmother, to the Georgia Colored Industrial School and Home in Macon, a boarding school run by Benjamin Bridges and his wife, Frances. Mr. and Mrs. Bridges were two upstanding African American educators in the community who believed strongly in shaping, molding, and teaching young people. Their school, located on a few acres of land, served both as a boarding school and an orphanage.

At the school, my grandmother Zetta not only excelled in reading, writing, and math, she became an avid violin player, mastering an instrument her mother, Georgia, learned to play as a student at Spelman Seminary. Zetta also developed an interest in painting and drawing, as well as a good relationship with classmate Augustus Brown, my grandfather. Zetta would watch August paint and draw birds, people, and houses. She even watched him build from scratch a model airplane that won first place at the Georgia Industrial School's annual spring fair in 1910.

For Zetta, the school was a boarding school; however, for August it was an orphanage. Both of his parents—his father, Calvin Brown, a shoemaker, and his mother, Mary—had died because of illness, and as a result Mr. and Mrs. Bridges, who were dear friends to his parents, took him in and continued as his parents would have, to expose him to culture while stressing education.

At the beginning of every school year, Mr. and Mrs. Bridges would have all the students dress in their very best: the girls would wear dresses and put pretty bows in their hair, and the boys would wear clean, pressed paints, jackets, and ties. Once dressed, the Bridgeses would have all the children and instructors go outside to have their pictures taken on the front lawn of the school building, in preparation of a brand-new school year. This annual ritual instilled pride and prepared students to take reading and writing, which was once illegal, seriously. Augustus and Zetta, my grandparents, said, "Learning always instilled freedom."

ARTICLE 27.

(1) Everyone has the right freely to participate in the cultural life of the community, to enjoy the arts and to share in scientific advancement and its benefits.
(2) Everyone has the right to the protection of the moral and material interests resulting from any scientific, literary or artistic production of which he is the author.

In the Family: Copyright Documents of Sadie Artis Wills

Betty Leacraft (Philadelphia, Pennsylvania), 2016.
50 × 50 inches; commercial and hand-dyed cotton, photo transfer, cotton batting; machine appliquéd, pieced, and quilted.

I am an exhibiting artist, and there are copyright laws existing in the United States that provide protection of my original artworks. These special laws prevent others from making copies, without my permission, of what is considered my "intellectual property." International copyright treaties also exist between the United States and participating nations around the world to protect my artworks whenever they are exhibited abroad. My quilt contains, as its focus, a copyright application, instructions, and a response letter from a copyright office for product labels my maternal grandmother received in 1947 for her "World's Wonder Hair Aid and Tetter Salve." These documents are an example of how far copyright has evolved since 1947. As a child, I helped stir pots of this product, moistened the copyrighted labels, and attached them to paper-backed metal container lids, then accompanied my grandmother to local beauty salons and the homes of individual customers who purchased her hair salve—one of several streams of income my grandmother created to help sustain a female-headed household.

ARTICLE 28.

Everyone is entitled to a social and international order in which the rights and freedoms set forth in this Declaration can be fully realized.

Carol Beck (Durham, North Carolina), 2016.
50 × 50 inches, commercial and hand-dyed cotton, photo transfer, cotton and wool batting, dimensional trapunto, embroidery, computer printing, fabric fusing, machine appliquéd and quilted.

Free as a Bird

The opportunity to express a childhood memory by using fabric was a challenging experience. This project brought back memories of being a ten-year-old girl assisting the teacher decorate the classroom. Our class had been studying the importance of documents. We learned that United Nations delegates were in Paris, France, discussing a human rights document that would affect people all over the world. I was very excited to learn that the "Universal Declaration of Human Rights" had been adopted by the United Nations General Assembly on December 10, 1948. My classmates and I did not realize or understand that children and adults around the world often did not have the same freedoms and rights we shared in the United States.

An international logo competition for the UN Human Rights Initiative was started in 2010. The goal was to design an original recognizable logo for the UN Human Rights movement. The *Free as a Bird* design was created by Predrag Stakic, a thirty-two-year-old artist from Serbia. His winning design was selected from 15,300-plus entries representing over 190 countries. His design combined the silhouette of a human hand as a bird in flight with a thumb grabbing the bird. Images of his logo were used on all four corners of my art quilt.

Created to Be Me

Cynthia Lockhart (Cincinnati, Ohio), 2016.
50 × 50 inches; multilayered assemblage of fabrics, recycled vintage fabric, hand-painted fabrics, upholstery textiles, lace, netting, and braids. In addition, accented with fibers, yarns, beading, and silkscreen patterning, as well as hand and machine quilting, bias French edging, draping, collage, and appliqué, including 3-D sculptural attributes.

My artwork *Free to Be Me* celebrates the spirit of Article 28 of the Universal Declaration of Human Rights. It states, "Everyone is entitled to a social and international order in which the rights and freedoms set forth in this Declaration can be fully realized."

At any given time in the history of humankind's journey, we see a pattern of a people who simply desired to provide for family, to survive, to be loved, to be safe, and to be treated fairly. These fundamental needs are universal and connect with all human beings. "In a Fair and Free World, there must be proper order so we can all enjoy rights and freedoms in our own country and all over the world," which is a quote from *Every Human Has Rights*, by Mary Robinson.

The visual imagery in the artwork represents a free spirit and celebrates the unending possibilities of the power of creativity. We all are human and have equal rights. We were born to dwell on this planet together and to contribute our talents and gifts to humankind in our unique ways. Each person is an original, one-of-a-kind blessing. God created everything. The diversity and inclusion of the races of people of different cultures is an essential component to the balance of our word. I love people of all races and ethnic backgrounds. We all have so much to contribute to society. Protecting each other's freedom is to protect your own freedom. This emotional connection is expressed through mixed fabrications of textures and elements. These elements have been shaped to depict the twists, curves, and bumps along the road of life.

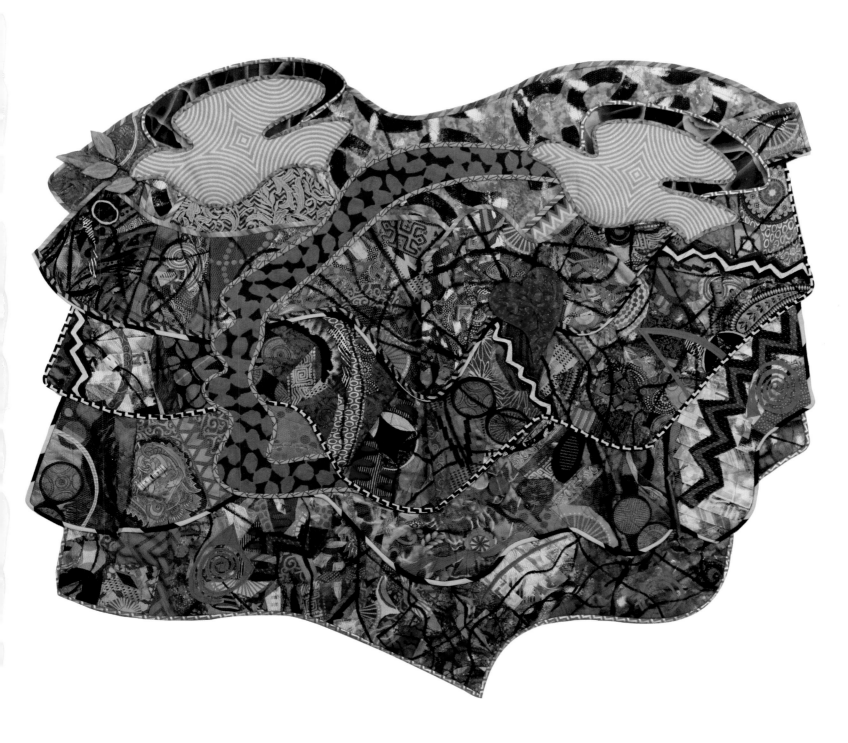

ARTICLE 29.

(1) Everyone has duties to the community in which alone the free
and full development of his personality is possible.

(2) In the exercise of his rights and freedoms, everyone shall be subject only to such
limitations as are determined by law solely for the purpose of securing due recognition
and respect for the rights and freedoms of others and of meeting the just requirements
of morality, public order and the general welfare in a democratic society.

(3) These rights and freedoms may in no case be exercised contrary to the purposes
and principles of the United Nations.

Every Man, Woman, and Child

Barbara McCraw (Denton, Texas), 2016.
50 × 50 inches, commercial and hand-dyed cotton, cotton batting,
machine and hand appliquéd, pieced, and machine and hand quilted.

The proposal for this quilt came to me at the same time that news programs were covering the hundreds of Middle Eastern refugees fleeing their war-torn homes. I saw families walking along dusty roads, hungry, thirsty, and trying to reach the rescue boats for safety. These people were African and Middle Eastern, seeking refuge in Greece and Europe. In the United States we had police killing unarmed African Americans. It occurred to me that we all are in the same boat, seeking freedom from violence in an effort to protect our families.

In this country, most of us are taught from an early age the tenets of the Bible. I believe that these same religious and human principles are taught around the world, whatever the faith. I remember reciting verses in which we learned how to be good and kind, considerate and compassionate, patient, tolerant, and helpful, but most of all responsible. Responsible not only at home, but in our communities and the world in which we live; to be good citizens to the earth and to each other.

I designed my quilt with inspiration from the escaping refugees, their boats overflowing with frightened people and rocking wildly from side to side. I chose to represent them as one man, one woman, and one child, sailing on a calm sea instead, and the ocean filled with ideas and hopes for all people. I believe that every person on this earth is entitled to these things, and I believe that we all are responsible for each other. When a society fails to feel responsibility for each other, we are doomed to fail. My quilt is a wish that we all travel the seas of hope and good will.

Responsibility: The Highest Aspiration of the People

Harriette Alford Meriwether (Pittsburgh, Pennsylvania), 2016.
50 × 50 inches, commercial cotton, photo transfer, cotton batting, machine appliquéd and quilted.

Article 29 of the Declaration of Human Rights declares that we have a duty and responsibility to other people to protect their rights and freedoms. We can do this by behaving ethically and with sustainable sensitivity. Organizations, associations, institutions, and the international community, all made up of people, should fulfill their solemn obligations to promote and encourage respect for human rights and the fundamental freedoms without distinctions of any kind, including distinctions based on race, color, sex, culture, occupation, language, environment, religion, politics or other opinions, national or social origin, education, economics, property, enterprise, entrepreneurship, birth or other status, and whatever it takes to fulfill the obligations of individual responsibility.

As an artist I envision that all people in the world would use their conscience and reasoning ability in support of human rights, for all people. People can make the difference, and if everyone did their part we could change the world. Herman Melville stated, "We cannot live for ourselves, a thousand fibers cannot connect us with our fellow men."

The silhouette profiles represent people everywhere—"red, yellow, black, and white," supporting the world because we have the duty and responsibility to promote, protect, and implement the rights and freedoms of all people. The world is done in trapunto-style quilting to accent the continents. The embroidered wording at the top captures the essence of some of the declaration we should embrace.

Simply, let's aspire to voluntarily eliminate irresponsible and unethical behaviors, which could bring serious harm to our global community, its people, or the environment, so that human rights can be fully realized

Responsibility

Sylvia Hernandez (Brooklyn, New York), 2016.
50 × 50 inches, commercial cotton, cotton batting,
machine appliquéd and quilted.

This quilt represents our responsibility to humanity and our planet. We should not just watch or record on social media the happenings of the world, but step up, educate, protest when necessary, and support one another on any number of issues. We must vote because it has not been given freely to all. Whenever we are afforded the opportunity to vote in an election, we should do so. VOTE! Each one teach one, so that the future might be brighter for the next generation.

Article 29

Ora Clay (Oakland, California), 2017.
50 × 50, commercial and batik cotton, machine
raw-edge appliqué, collage, machine quilted.

Article 29 addresses our duty to care for other people and protect their rights and freedoms. The theme of my quilt is the responsibility we have to ensure that all people have access to clean water.

The background of the quilt is composed of varying shades of fused blue fabrics, used to depict the feeling of water. The quilting is done with silk and cotton blue variegated threads for a heightened visual effect.

Older children often have the responsibility of taking care of their younger siblings. As the eldest of six siblings, I learned the meaning of responsibility at an early age. Growing up, I was often left "in charge." This meant I was responsible for my sisters and brothers while my parents were away. I understood that it was my responsibility to keep them safe and provide what they needed until my parents returned.

The children I created in the quilt were inspired by a photo taken by Nicholas Kristof in 2011 during the Somalia famine. He explained, "In the area where new refugees gathered to register at Oadaab, the small child on the right was thirsty, so an older child picked up a jerry can and offered him a drink of water."

But our responsibility goes beyond individuals with whom we have a relationship. In his speech "Conquering Self-Centeredness," on August 11, 1957, Dr. Martin Luther King Jr. said, "An individual has not started living fully until they can rise above the narrow confines of individualistic concerns to the broader concerns of humanity. . . . This is the judgment. Life's most persistent and urgent question is, What are you doing for others?"

Dr. Mona Hanna-Attisha in Flint, Michigan, demonstrated her responsibility by exposing the fact that the lead-contaminated water being delivered to homes will adversely affect children for years to come. Flint is just one place; however, clean water is a universal right, and our collective responsibility is to ensure that all have access to it.

Many of the officials in Flint did not exercise responsible behavior. Not only did they not protect the residents of Flint, or remedy the contaminated water situation, they initially ordered clean, bottled water for their offices and not for the residents.

"Every person must decide at some point, whether they will walk in the light of creative altruism or in the darkness of destructive selfishness." —Martin Luther King Jr.

ARTICLE 30.

Nothing in this Declaration may be interpreted as implying for any State, group or person any right to engage in any activity or to perform any act aimed at the destruction of any of the rights and freedoms set forth herein.

The Right to Say No More

Bisa Butler (West Orange, New Jersey), 2016.
50 × 50 inches, commercial and hand-dyed cotton, acrylic paint, cotton batting, hand painting, machine appliquéd and quilted.

My quilt focuses on an image of a young boy with a hood on his head, which evokes the deeply disturbing story of Trayvon Martin. In 2012 Trayvon Martin was murdered while wearing a hoodie, and since his murder the hoodie is embedded in our cultural lexicon to represent a young, unarmed black man. He, like Emmett Till, was killed for doing nothing more than going about his business. Both young boys were unarmed, and both were brutally taken away from this world by racists. Trayvon Martin was walking home from a convenience store, wearing a dark hooded sweatshirt and carrying a bag that contained a can of Arizona Iced Tea and a bag of Skittles candy. He looked suspicious to a local neighborhood watch volunteer. As an African American, I know it was the color of Trayvon's skin that aroused suspicion. In the small, racist mind of the neighborhood watch volunteer, Trayvon had no right to walk around that neighborhood without his "permission." Trayvon was attacked and beaten and was shot in cold blood because he refused to be interrogated by the neighborhood watch person. Both Trayvon's and Emmett Till's murderers were never convicted. Their deaths remain stains on the collective consciousness of the American people.

The figure in my quilt shows a young man with a hoodie, who could be Trayvon, or he could be someone else. He is all of our sons. Behind him is the city, the concrete jungle that surrounds so many of our urban centers. We are human beings. Our ancestors were Africans who were connected to the land, yet we are surrounded by manmade slabs of concrete and glass. In the image, the gray-and-white buildings dwarf the figure and are endless. The image of the colorful man-child surrounded by the city is framed by depictions of clouds and green grass. All of the things that should be afforded to us: clean air, freedom, the right to move, happiness, the right to live carefree. This piece represents that essential right to life, the right to walk unmolested, the right to say silent if we feel like it, the right to fight when we are attacked, and the right not to be killed while we are walking home from the store. The rights taken away from Trayvon Martin and Emmett Till are still important today, and my quilt is a reminder of that truth. The figure stares out at us, because what happened then still happens now. We have a right to stand up and say, "no more!"

183

Weather the Storm: My Body, My Choice

Earamichia Brown (New York, New York), 2017.
36 × 27 inches, commercial cotton, silk, cotton batting, leather fabrics, Mistyfuse, fused, machine appliquéd and quilted.

I originally began this piece in hopes of witnessing the election of this nation's first female president. It was going to symbolize the breaking of the glass ceiling. However, it has become a symbol of the storm that women under the 45th administration are facing. We as women have to shield ourselves from the shards of the 45th administration's policies affecting a woman's right to choose. This administration is moving swiftly to roll back the reproductive freedom of women. From the defunding of Planned Parenthood to the push to ban abortion, a woman's right to choose is under attack.

On January 21, 2017, women gathered together in Washington, DC, and in cities across the country and the world to march for women's rights. I was in DC for the march and noticed that a large number of the signs were about women's right to choose and about owning their own bodies. Some of the signs said "Resistance is Fertile," and others made reference to their ovaries and the need for *Roe v. Wade*. Ownership of our bodies was the prevailing theme for the day. Controlling our bodies is key to our ability to be economically free.

In April, Trump signed legislation aimed at cutting off federal funding to Planned Parenthood and other groups that perform abortions. Unfortunately, this nullifies a rule that the Obama administration completed during its last days that effectively barred state and local governments from withholding federal funding for family-planning services related to contraception, sexually transmitted infections, fertility, pregnancy care, and breast and cervical cancer screening from qualified health providers—regardless of whether they also performed abortions. The new measure cleared Congress in March, with Vice President Mike Pence casting the tie-breaking vote in the Senate.

The gale-force winds of the 45th administration will continue to wreak havoc on our rights as women, but we must continue to fight for our bodies and ourselves. The storm is raging around us, and we must continue to resist.

Jacqueline Dukes (Shaker Heights, Ohio), 2016.
50 × 50 inches, commercial cotton, photo transfer, cotton batting,
machine appliquéd and quilted.

By participating in this project I seek to align myself with those who care for the future of humanity. It is my belief that in lending our voices to this cause, hearts will be touched, and reflection upon the way we treat each other will occur. Perhaps meaningful conversations will begin, because the issues presented in the work resonate with viewers of this exhibit.

Because I am committed to everyone having the right for a good quality of life that enables them to thrive, I can accept the strengths of the Universal Declaration of Human Rights while understanding the biases and problematic assumptions that are contained within. That's my reality, but in order for these possibilities to exist in numerous other places, those groups will need to examine their own political and religious expectations. Each nation must sort these problems out, though outsiders may become impatient. When foreigners interfere, mayhem usually occurs. In an ideal world, I believe that if everyone had the ability to live their daily lives in the manner of their choice, it is more productive than the ongoing fight for self-determination. How these tenets are incorporated into a society has yet to be resolved in most countries.

I chose Article 30 because it declares that recommended rights have been defined, and there is an expectation that all of the first twenty-nine articles are to remain as stated. No one article dismisses or overrides another. The background fabric is cotton from Africa—birthplace of all. The prints for the number 30 are about music and community, which is universal. The textiles were selected because the designs embody movement, and due to conditions in their homelands, many people are mobile, whether by choice or not. The colors were chosen because they represent all the major ethnic groups of the world. I was influenced by the lyrics of the famous hymn, "Jesus loves the little children—all the children of the world. Red and yellow, black and white, they are precious in his sight." One need not be religious to accept that everybody matters simply because they exist. Included are pictures from world cultures, plus the Chinese symbol for "people" is embroidered in several places along the "30." Most of the work is machine pieced and stitched. Metal buttons with words of affirmation have been attached to reinforce hopes and dreams for the future. Article 30 reconfirms that all the rights are inalienable!

I am the voice behind the tears that fill the ... *intimate*

Allow me to honor and comfort you ... *my art so that you will always know you* ... have a voice.

Silent No More is a

reminder that no one can take away your

Human Rights

U.N. DECLARATION FOR HUMAN RIGHTS #30

No One Can Take Your Human Rights

Celestine Butler (Omaha, Nebraska), 2017.
50 × 50 inches, commercial and hand-dyed cotton, crystals, cotton batting, machine appliquéd, machine quilting.

Drawing inspiration from the words in the UN Declaration of Human Rights, Article 30, which clearly states "No One Can Take Away Your Human Rights," this quilt was birthed from my vision to create the feeling of a universal cosmic atmosphere. The words we speak into the universe have power, even when no one else is present to hear them. The innocent yet sincere whispers of our prayers fill the atmosphere. The crystals streaming down the face of the silhouette represent the many tears we shed in the places where we feel alone. Savannah E. C. Devereaux, age eleven, was the subject for the silhouette. I wrote and screen-printed the words to breathe and speak life for all human rights. The floating strings of lights symbolize words and prayers spoken in silence around the world for human rights. Her hands are clasped to prayer to remind us to hold human rights close to the heart and in all of our thoughts and prayers.

End Child Marriage

Sandra Johnson (Orange, California), 2017.
50 × 50 inches, batik cotton, printing on cotton,
cotton batting, machine pieced and quilted.

In many ways, the twentieth century was defined by the move for civil rights. Among these was the fight for the equal rights of women. In many countries the rights of a woman are protected by laws; however, there are still countries that hold historical rights of the man over the woman. The hope of a young girl to be able to live out her dreams are stopped once she is married off. Gender inequality, poverty, tradition, and insecurity fuel child marriage.

Child marriage is more prevalent in countries with higher rates of poverty and a lack of education and are ingrained in cultural practices. Through this quilt, I wanted to remind us all that these young girls have a voice. The girls in this piece are standing with signs to express their frustration. The first sign is a call to action, "End Child Marriage." We all can do our part to end this practice. Understanding the "Life Long Consequences" to child marriage will help educate the world to the higher likelihood of violence in the marriage, as well as sexually transmitted disease and health problems for the young bride. We must challenge gender inequality. The third sign, "Marriage and Family," simply states the right of women to get married when and to whom we want. The fifth and final sign calls on specific countries to take action.

The use of bright colors such as red, yellow, and blue communicate to the viewer happiness and hope. Denim was used for the quilt's scalloped boarder. It reminds me of the past, when the slaves had denim overalls.

Marriage can make a young girl feel like a slave, in the sense that she is now responsible for cooking, cleaning, raising the children, and tending to her new family in their old age.

Understand that human rights include the rights inherent to *all* human beings and are not dependent on our nationality, our place of residence, sex, color, religion, language, or any other status. We all are eligible and deserving of our human rights without discrimination.

One way to help move toward solving this complex problem is to help empower young girls and educating them on their rights. This piece of art was created to empower all of us to act against child marriage by spreading awareness with the hope of a brighter future for all.

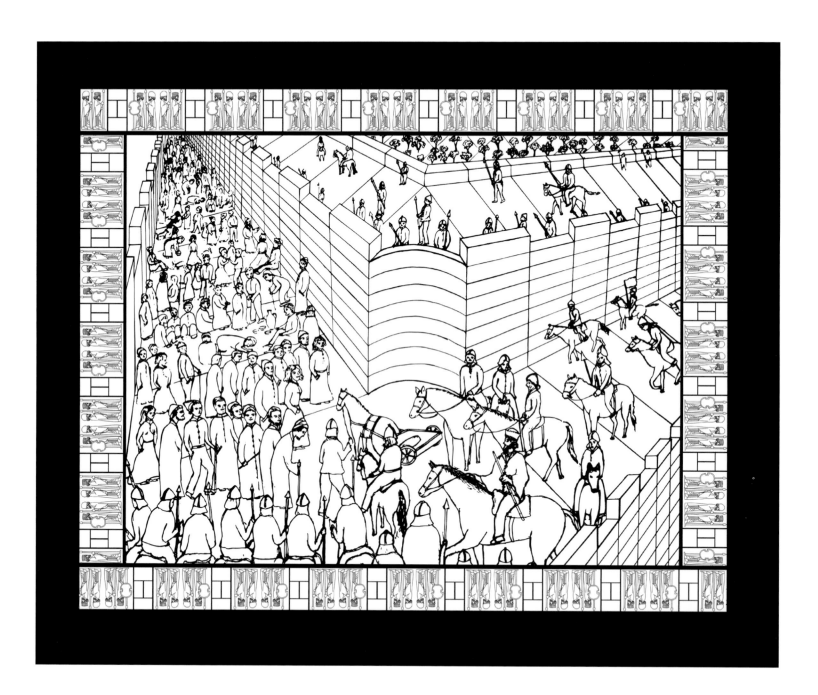

The Dawn of Human Rights

Behrooz Assani (Liberty Township, Ohio), 2017. 50 × 50 inches, printed on cotton, cotton batting, machine quilted.

Cyrus the Great, known as Kourosh to the Persians, was the first king of the Achaemenid Empire. He was known to many at the time as a peace bringer and liberator. In around 539 BCE, King Cyrus marched into the city of Babylon with his army and conquered it. The account was inscribed in Akkadian on a cylinder of clay, now known as the Cyrus Cylinder.

According to the cylinder, Nabonidus, the last king of Babylon, was a weak and corrupted leader who enslaved his people. In response to this, Marduk, the patron god of Babylon, abandoned the city in anger. Marduk searched the lands for another young man to take over the Babylonian kingdom, which is when he came across Cyrus. He saw Cyrus as a righteous man and decided to hand over the Babylonian kingdom to him. Cyrus walked into Babylon with Marduk at his side and, without any battle or conflict, overthrew Nabonidus. The cylinder transcribes the king's liberation of all the enslaved people, and how he let them return to their homelands. King Cyrus believed that it was his duty to create peace among his kingdom. The Jews praised Cyrus because he allowed them to return to Palestine. Everyone was allowed to follow their own way of life, as well as worship any god of their choosing. King Cyrus also ordered the reconstruction of all the destroyed temples in Babylon. This type of ruling was unheard of at the time, because conquering a land meant that the victors would own the people as well. Instead, Cyrus showed support of the people and their culture. Due to this, King Cyrus gained overwhelming support throughout his empire for his kind and merciful way of ruling.

From the moment it was excavated in 1879, to its current home in the British Museum in London, the Cyrus Cylinder has always been seen as a symbol of human rights. The major ideas captured by the cylinder are based on the notion that every human has basic freedoms. These include the right to practice a chosen religion, the right to compensation in return for work, and the freedom to migrate to a specific homeland. Also, it captures the idea that there is equality between all different races, even under the rule of the same empire. These principles are, even today, considered to be basic human liberties, as seen in the first chapter of the Charter of Human Rights and Freedoms. In fact, a replica of the cylinder can be found on display on the second floor of the United Nations headquarters in New York City, because it promotes the concept of freedom of the people. The Iranians embrace the cylinder as a reminder of the culture of tolerance, humanity, and freedom created by Cyrus the Great. However, for the future, the cylinder can, I hope, serve as more than just a reminder, but also as an example.

Index of Artists

Carolyn L. Mazloomi is among the most influential historians of African American quilts in the United States. Mazloomi is the recipient of the 2014 Bess Lomax Hawes NEA National Heritage Fellowship Award, the highest honor our nation bestows upon its folk and traditional artists, and the Ohio Heritage Fellowship. She was inducted into the Quilters Hall of Fame in 2016 and has written eight books on African American quilts, including *And Still We Rise: Race, Culture, and Visual Conversations.* She is the founder of Women of Color Quilters Network. Widely exhibited in the United States and internationally, Mazloomi's artwork can be found in the Smithsonian Institution's American Museum of Art, the National Civil Rights Museum, the Mint Museum, the American Museum of Art and Design, and the Wadsworth Atheneum Museum. She has been recognized by the International Labour Department in Geneva and by the United Nations for her work to help advance women.

www.carolynlmazloomi.com | www.wcqn.org